Y SERVICE

Estate

557126

KT-405-371

my kitchen

James Martin

my kitchen
James Martin

CHESHIRE
LIBRARIES

2 6 MAY 2010

R2

Collins

Contents

GARDEN

Introduction

"It's all in a season." That's what my granddad used to say to me. A keen gardener, he would to take me to his allotment and greenhouse whenever I went to visit. That was my first real insight into fresh food and where it comes from – before that it had just been microwaved jacket potatoes or steak with onion rings from a Berni Inn. So, I'm sure it was there – right there – aged five, that the seeds were planted in my mind, and I knew I was going to be a cook.

Many people in the UK grow up in urban areas with little or no awareness of where their food comes from and when it is actually in season. In my opinion, this is mainly down to the supermarkets offering the same food week-in, week-out. But the seasons are the planet's natural cycle and they exist for a reason, so it makes no sense to try and beat them. Think of each changing season as 'out with the old and in with the new', welcome the next lot of produce and don't go searching for out-of-season food. There are so many good reasons to eat what we produce locally, the obvious ones being to support the British farmers, to reduce CO_2 emissions from transport, and above all else to get the best possible taste. You only have to try Jersey Royals or British strawberries to understand what I mean.

In a country obsessed with cheaper and cheaper food, we should take a step back and re-assess. If we want great food on our plates we have to be willing to pay for it. I'm not saying it has to be expensive – we're still talking pence, not pounds and, in fact, food is at its cheapest when in season – even luxury foods like asparagus. Things are already changing for the better, with people learning more about food from books and TV programmes and paying closer attention to what they are eating. But more can still be done. We just need to get out of the habit of expecting what we want whenever we want it. It has always been my mission to champion the food that's on our doorstep, and this is exactly the food I cook at home, in my own kitchen.

Those who have their own garden or allotment will always have access to the utmost in fresh produce. They will also know that it's a great teaching tool for young and old alike, and that growing your own food can be a source of much satisfaction. Most importantly, if we eat seasonal food it will be at its cheapest because of its abundance, and the flavour will be at its best. This book is all about celebrating this island of ours, and the food that grows on it, and the best way I can get you excited about cooking this way in your own home is to give you the recipes I cook in my own throughout the year.

Enjoy,

James

Spring

Radishes • Asparagus • Spring onions • Leeks
Jerusalem artichokes • Spinach • Elderflowers
Rhubarb • Parsley • Lamb • Sea bass • Salmon

Spring brings a garden to life with the promise of delicious crops to come. In Britain we can enjoy seasonal produce such as wild garlic, Jerusalem artichokes and watercress. Radishes and spring onions push up through the soil and elderflowers fill the hedgerows. Sea bass and salmon are a real treat for seafood lovers, while for meat eaters the end of the season brings with it succulent spring lamb. And I wouldn't be a true Yorkshireman if I didn't mention the best bit of all – rhubarb! Harvest from the garden or enjoy the tender pink forced variety, still available at this time of year.

Spring onion potato cakes with fried duck eggs

Serves 4
Vegetarian

4 large floury potatoes, peeled and quartered
½ bunch of spring onions, finely chopped
2 tbsp chopped chives
110g (4oz) flour, for dusting
150ml (5fl oz) olive oil
110g (4oz) butter
4 duck eggs
200g (7oz) watercress
50ml (2fl oz) extra-virgin olive oil
20ml (¾fl oz) white wine vinegar
Salt and black pepper

Potato cakes are excellent as a starter or as a filling snack. They can be prepared in advance and kept in the fridge until needed. Duck eggs are a Saturday Kitchen *favourite. Cook them just like hens' eggs; however, they're too rich to use in baking.*

Place the potatoes in a large saucepan, cover with water and add a good pinch of salt. Bring to the boil and cook for 20–25 minutes, then drain and return to the pan. With the pan on a heatproof surface, mash the potatoes well, then transfer to a large bowl and season with salt and pepper. Mix in the spring onions and chives and divide the mixture into eight balls.

Lightly dust a work surface with flour, place a potato ball on it and shape into a round, flat cake about 1cm (½in) thick and 5cm (2in) wide. Repeat with the rest of the potato and place the finished cakes in the fridge for about an hour to firm up.

Add the olive oil to a non-stick frying pan, dust the potato cakes with flour and fry over a medium heat for 3–4 minutes on each side. Depending on the size of the pan, you may have to cook them in batches.

While the potato cakes are cooking, melt the butter in another non-stick frying pan, set over a medium heat, and once it is hot and bubbling, crack the duck eggs into the pan and cook them until the edges are crispy but the centres remain soft.

Dress the watercress with the extra-virgin olive oil and the vinegar and season with salt and pepper, to your taste. Place 1–2 potato cakes on each plate, top with a fried egg, drizzle with the leftover butter from the egg pan and serve with some watercress on the side.

Cream of Jerusalem artichoke soup with bacon

Serves 4

300g (11oz) Jerusalem artichokes
1 large shallot
1 small potato
4 tbsp extra-virgin olive oil
1 clove of garlic, peeled and crushed
500ml (18fl oz) Vegetable Stock (see page 218)
3 rashers of smoked streaky bacon
110ml (4fl oz) double cream
Salt and black pepper
Crusty bread, to serve

Jerusalem artichokes are the roots of a plant related to the sunflower. They come into season very early in spring, sometimes even earlier, at the tail end of winter. Despite having the same name, the globe artichoke comes from a completely different plant and isn't in season until the summer. Jerusalem artichokes make excellent soup; I also love them in purées, salads or simply sautéed.

Peel the artichokes, shallot and potato and chop into 1cm (½in) cubes. Set a large, heavy-based saucepan over a medium heat and add 2 tablespoons of olive oil. Tip in the vegetables and fry gently for 2–3 minutes, without browning.

Add the garlic and pour in the vegetable stock. Bring to the boil and cook for 8–10 minutes or until the artichokes and potato are cooked through and soft.

Meanwhile, heat the grill to high and grill the bacon on both sides until crispy, then set aside. Once cool, cut into pieces.

Add the cream to the soup, bring back up to the boil and cook for another 2–3 minutes. Remove the pan from the heat, then pour the soup into a blender and purée until smooth. Alternatively, purée the soup using a held-held blender.

Return the soup to the pan, reheat gently and add salt and pepper, to taste. Pour the soup into bowls and sprinkle with small pieces of the bacon. Drizzle with the remaining olive oil and serve with fresh crusty bread.

Frisée, radish and orange salad

Serves 4
Vegetarian

3 oranges
½ head frisée lettuce
4 radishes, sliced
½ bunch of chives, in
    2.5cm (1in) lengths
1 tbsp white wine
    vinegar
5 tbsp extra-virgin
    olive oil
Salt and black pepper

This refreshing salad makes a great accompaniment to fish, especially smoked salmon. The outer leaves of frisée lettuce can be bitter, so use the inner leaves only.

Zest two oranges, then peel and break the segments into a large bowl. Add the lettuce leaves, radish slices and chives.

To make the dressing, put the zest in another bowl with the juice of the third orange and the vinegar. Whisk in the olive oil and season with salt and pepper.

Pour the dressing over the salad, toss the leaves to coat evenly and serve immediately.

Bibb lettuce salad with radishes

Serves 4
Vegetarian

4 heads of Bibb lettuce
6 tbsp chopped mixed
    fresh herbs
2 shallots
8 radishes
1 tbsp Dijon mustard
2 tbsp red wine vinegar
5 tbsp rapeseed oil
Salt and black pepper

A simple salad, ideal with grilled chicken or fish. If you can't get Bibb lettuce, use Little Gem instead; and feel free to replace the rapeseed oil with a good-quality extra-virgin olive oil.

Cut away the base section from each lettuce and place the leaves in a large bowl. Add all the herbs to the bowl and mix well together. Peel and thinly slice the shallots, slice the radishes and layer both with the salad leaves onto plates.

In a separate bowl, mix together the mustard and vinegar and slowly add the rapeseed or olive oil. Season well with salt and pepper, drizzle the dressing over the salad leaves and serve.

Montgomery cheese balls with rosemary

Serves 4
Vegetarian

450ml (16fl oz) milk
125g (4½oz)
  Montgomery's
  Cheddar or any
  good-quality, mature
  Cheddar cheese
20g (¾oz) butter, plus
  extra for greasing
150g (5oz) plain flour
2 whole eggs, beaten
6 eggs, separated into
  whites and yolks
2 tbsp finely chopped
  rosemary leaves
300g (11oz) dried
  breadcrumbs, such
  as Japanese panko
1.2 litres (2 pints)
  vegetable oil, for
  deep-frying
Salt and black pepper

These are excellent as canapés, as a starter or, in larger quantities, as a vegetarian main course. Serve simply with salad, such as the Bibb Lettuce Salad with Radishes (see page 13).

Gently warm the milk in a small saucepan over a low heat – do not let it boil. Grate the cheese into a bowl and set aside.

Place the butter, flour, beaten eggs and the six yolks in a large saucepan, add the grated cheese and set over a low heat. Gradually add the warm milk, stirring continuously with a whisk to prevent lumps. Once all of the milk has been added, keep stirring until the mixture begins to thicken.

When the mixture starts to come away from the sides of the pan, season with salt and pepper and pour out on to a greased baking tray to cool. Once cool, mould the mixture into balls each about the size of a golf ball and place in the fridge for 30 minutes to firm up.

Beat the egg whites in a bowl and mix the rosemary and breadcrumbs in another bowl. Dip the cheese balls first into the egg white, then the rosemary breadcrumbs and either cook straight away or return to the fridge and cook later.

If using a deep-fat fryer, heat the vegetable oil to 190°C (375°F). Alternatively, fill a deep, heavy-based frying pan to a depth of 2cm (¾in) with oil and use a sugar thermometer to check that it has reached the correct temperature.

Remove the balls from the fridge and lower into the fryer or pan. Cook for 4–5 minutes until golden brown, then carefully lift out with a slotted spoon, drain on kitchen paper and serve.

Seared sea bass with blood orange and spring onion salad

Serves 4

4 blood oranges
1 bunch of spring onions, cut into 2.5cm (1in) lengths
200g (7oz) mixed salad leaves
1 tbsp olive oil
4 x 125g (4½oz) sea bass fillets, all bones removed
1 bunch of basil, leaves only
Salt and black pepper

For the dressing
25ml (1fl oz) white wine vinegar
Pinch of caster sugar
110ml (4fl oz) extra-virgin olive oil

Farmed sea bass has become widely available in recent years, but if you can get hold of line-caught bass it's definitely worth the extra cost. Blood oranges are a beautiful deep red colour and have a much more distinctive flavour than regular oranges (although you could use these as an alternative). They go well in savoury dishes and salads.

Peel three of the oranges and break the segments into a large bowl along with the spring onions. Season with salt and pepper, then add the salad leaves and toss together. Set aside.

To make the dressing, squeeze the juice from the remaining orange into another bowl and mix with the vinegar and sugar. Whisk in the extra-virgin olive oil until fully incorporated. Drizzle a little of the dressing over the prepared salad and toss together to coat.

Pour the olive oil into a non-stick frying pan set over a high heat. Place the sea bass fillets in the pan, skin side down, and sear for 3–4 minutes or until the sides of the fish start to brown. Turn over, cook for 1 more minute, add half the basil and remove from the heat, keeping the fish in the pan to allow them to carry on cooking in the residual heat. Set aside.

Divide the salad between plates, then lift the sea bass fillets from the pan and place on top of the salad. Scatter with the remaining basil, drizzle over the rest of the dressing and serve.

Dill-marinated salmon with lime and rhubarb salad

Serves 4

**2 sticks of rhubarb,
 any leaves removed**
**25g (1oz) pickled
 ginger, finely
 chopped, and juice**
Zest and juice of 1 lime
**50ml (2fl oz) extra-
 virgin olive oil**
**15g (½oz) chives,
 chopped**
**2 x 250g packets of
 dill-marinated
 salmon or smoked
 salmon**
Salt and black pepper
**1 lemon, cut into
 wedges, to serve**
Crusty bread, to serve

My chef, Chris, came up with this idea while experimenting in the kitchen. I liked the combination of these ingredients so much that I put it on the menu at my bistro. If you can't find dill-marinated salmon, just use regular smoked salmon instead.

Thinly slice the rhubarb lengthways and cut into very fine sticks, the size of matchsticks. Place in a bowl of iced water and leave for 20 minutes.

Place the pickled ginger and juice in a bowl, add the lime zest and juice along with the olive oil, then season, to taste, with salt and pepper.

Remove the rhubarb from the iced water, mix into the bowl with the dressing and stir in the chives. Slice up the salmon and arrange on a board or platter, or divide between plates. Serve with the rhubarb salad, some lemon wedges to squeeze over the salmon, and chunks of crusty bread on the side.

Grilled halibut with champ and lemon caper butter

Serves 4

500g (1lb 2oz) floury potatoes, peeled and cut into quarters
110ml (4fl oz) milk
50g (2oz) butter
150g (5oz) spring onions, chopped
4 x 150g (5oz) halibut fillets, all bones removed
1 tbsp olive oil
110g (4oz) caper berries or capers
Peeled segments of 4 lemons, plus the juice of 1 lemon
1 tbsp chopped flat-leaf parsley
Salt and black pepper

Halibut is a meaty fish, full of flavour and with very few bones. If you can't get caper berries, use small capers (caper buds) instead, but if they're in salt or brine, rinse well in hot water before using.

Put the potatoes in a large saucepan, cover with water and add a good pinch of salt. Bring to the boil and cook for 20–25 minutes, then drain the potatoes and return to the pan, which should no longer be over the heat.

Pour the milk into a small saucepan and heat until nearly boiling. Crush the potatoes with a fork or potato masher until they form a chunky mash, then slowly add the hot milk, stirring all the time.

Melt half the butter in a frying pan over a medium heat, tip in the spring onions and sauté for about 2 minutes. Add these to the mash, then season well with salt and pepper and set aside.

Season the halibut with salt and pepper and drizzle with olive oil. Place in a non-stick frying pan over a high heat and cook for 3–4 minutes on each side, or until the fish starts to turn golden-brown. Remove from the heat and set aside.

Add the remaining butter to a medium-sized saucepan set over a high heat. When it has turned nut brown in colour, add the caper berries and the juice of one lemon. Season, then remove from the heat and add the lemon segments and parsley.

Place some champ on each plate with a piece of halibut at the side. Spoon the lemon caper butter over the top and serve.

Mackerel with caramelised radishes

Serves 4

16 baby white onions, peeled and left whole
16 radishes
1 tbsp runny honey
2 tsp cumin seeds
4 mackerel, gutted and washed
2 banana shallots, peeled and sliced
2 lemons, sliced
1 bunch of coriander
1 bunch of chives
½ bunch of thyme
50ml (2fl oz) olive oil

This recipe was inspired by a trip to France, where I visited a great market right on the seafront. The fishing boats were moored up alongside the market stalls, which were laden with fresh fish – in particular, mackerel, which is unbeatable when eaten fresh and cooked simply. I was also impressed by the crisp, vibrant radishes on sale. Here I've found a way to combine the two.

Place the onions and 110ml (4fl oz) water in a large non-stick saucepan. Bring to the boil and allow to cook for 5 minutes, or until tender, then add the radishes and cook for a further 2–3 minutes.

Add the honey and cumin seeds and cook for a further 5–6 minutes. The colour of the radishes will gradually start to run and form a glaze. When nearly all the liquid has evaporated, remove the pan from the heat.

Preheat the oven to 180°C (350°F), Gas 4. To prepare the mackerel, place 4 sheets of foil on a work surface – each sheet about the size of a newspaper. Divide the shallots, lemons and herbs between the pieces of foil, placing a pile in the middle of each sheet. Place the mackerel on top and score the fish with a sharp knife. Drizzle with the olive oil and a tablespoon of water and fold the foil over to form small parcels.

Place the parcels on a baking tray, put in the oven and cook for about 8–10 minutes. Remove from the oven, open up the parcels and transfer the fish to plates. Gently reheat the onion and radish mix, divide between the plates and serve.

Cod with clams, curly kale and wild garlic

Serves 4

**4 tbsp rapeseed or
   extra-virgin olive oil**
150g (5oz) butter
**4 x 150g (5oz) cod
   fillets, skin on**
**400g (14oz) small,
   fresh clams, in shells**
**2 shallots, peeled and
   finely chopped**
**200ml (7fl oz) perry
   (cider-like drink
   made from pears) or
   cider**
**225g (8oz) curly kale,
   stalks discarded**
**110g (4oz) wild garlic
   leaves, or 110g (4oz)
   fresh spinach and
   2 cloves of garlic,
   peeled and chopped**
Zest of 1 lemon
**3 tsp finely chopped
   chives**
Salt and black pepper

When buying cod, go for thicker fillets from larger fish, as these have the best flavour and don't break up too much during cooking. Wild garlic can be found in woodland and by the side of the road; the leaves should be picked before the heads flower. If you can't find it, use spinach and chopped cloves of garlic instead.

Preheat the oven to 190°C (375°F), Gas 5. Set an ovenproof pan or roasting tin on the hob over a high heat and, when the pan is hot, add the rapeseed or olive oil and 25g (1oz) butter. When the butter has melted, fry the cod fillets for 2–3 minutes on each side, until they are golden-brown all over.

Transfer the pan to the oven and roast the fish for 5 minutes until just cooked through. Remove the pan from the oven, cover with foil and set aside to rest.

Meanwhile, put the clams in a colander and wash thoroughly under running water, discarding any with broken shells or those that don't close when they are tapped against the side of the colander.

Set a large saucepan over a high heat and, when hot, add the clams, shallots and most of the perry or cider. Lower the heat and simmer, uncovered, for 2–3 minutes, until the clams have opened and the liquid has slightly reduced.

Clean out the colander and place it over a similar-sized bowl. Pour the clams and cooking liquid into the colander so that the liquid drains through to the bowl. Return the liquid to the pan and set the clams aside. Discard any which haven't opened during cooking.

Bring the liquid to the boil and cook until reduced and thickened. To finish the sauce, add half of the remaining butter to the pan and whisk to combine. Season with salt and pepper and then keep it warm until you are ready to serve the dish.

Bring a large saucepan of salted water to the boil and add the curly kale. Cook for 2–3 minutes until just tender. Drain the kale well and place in a frying pan. Add the remaining butter, wild garlic leaves (or spinach and garlic) and lemon zest, and cook over a medium–high heat for just 20 seconds, to wilt the wild garlic. Season with salt and pepper, to taste.

To serve, divide the kale and wild garlic leaves between plates and place the cod on top. Add the final splash of perry and the chives to the clam sauce. Then spoon some of the mixture over the cod and arrange the clams on top. Pour the remaining sauce over the fish and clams, and serve.

Trout with green beans and almonds

Serves 4

4 fresh trout, gutted but with the heads left on
150g (5oz) butter, melted
75g (3oz) whole, shelled almonds
300g (11oz) French beans, topped and tailed
Salt and black pepper

With trendy new varieties of fish arriving from all over the world, we tend to forget how good our own locally-sourced species can be. Trout is a prime example – it's available all year round and, served with almonds, it's a classic fish dish.

Place each trout on its back and open up the ribcage with a knife. Using sharp kitchen scissors, cut the backbone in two places – at the highest point near the head and the lowest point by the tail. If you prefer, you can ask your fishmonger to do this for you.

Preheat the oven to 200°C (400°F), Gas 6. Brush each fish, inside and out, with half the butter and season with salt and pepper. Butter a roasting tin and place the fish in the tin, pressing each one down with its ribcage pointing up.

Bake in the oven for 6 minutes and then add the almonds to the tin. Cook for a further 5–6 minutes, then remove from the oven. You can tell when the fish is cooked when you can pull out the backbone easily. Do this for all four fish.

While the fish is cooking, bring a saucepan of salted water to the boil, add the beans and cook for 4–5 minutes, or until just tender. Drain the beans and place in a warmed bowl.

Place the fish on plates and add the remaining butter to the hot roasting tin. Remove the almonds from the tin and add to the beans. Season well with salt and pepper. To serve, place the beans and almonds into the cavity of each trout and spoon over the hot butter from the tin.

Wok-fried chicken with ginger, chilli and wild garlic

Serves 4

4 x 175g (6oz) boneless, skinless chicken breasts
4 tbsp cornflour
1 tbsp corn oil
2 tbsp finely chopped root ginger
6 spring onions, sliced on the diagonal into 2cm (¾in) pieces
1 red chilli, finely chopped
2 bunches of wild garlic leaves or 225g bag of baby spinach
1 clove of garlic, peeled and chopped
4 tbsp dark soy sauce
Salt
Steamed rice, to serve

The chicken in this recipe is coated in cornflour and poached in water, a cooking method known as 'velveting'. Pork can be done in the same way. It's great for a stir-fry, in which the meat is cooked quite quickly, because it really does help to give it a softer texture.

Place a large wok or non-stick frying pan and a large saucepan of salted water on the hob, both set over a high heat. While they are heating, slice the chicken breasts thinly.

Coat the chicken pieces in the cornflour, then place in the water, once it has come to the boil, and blanch for 2 minutes. Remove the chicken from the water and set aside.

Add the corn oil to the wok or frying pan, followed by the chicken, ginger, spring onions and chilli, mixing well together. Cook for 1 minute, then add the remaining ingredients and season with a pinch of salt. Cook for about 1 minute, or until the wild garlic or spinach leaves wilt down.

Serve in bowls with helpings of steamed rice.

Sautéed chicken livers and mushrooms on toast

Serves 4

4 slices from a white bloomer
30g (1¼oz) butter
6 rashers of back bacon, cut into lardons
400g (14oz) chicken livers
200g (7oz) brown cap mushrooms, cut in half
50ml (2fl oz) white wine
110ml (4fl oz) double cream
3 tbsp chopped flat-leaf parsley
Salt and black pepper

Chicken livers are one of the few remaining inexpensive meats and we should use them in cooking a lot more than we do. Make sure the green parts of the livers are removed and don't overcook them or they will become bitter-tasting and grainy. Mushrooms and double cream make this dish smooth and rich, a perfect opposite to the crunchy toast.

Toast the bread either in a toaster or under the grill, preheated to medium–high, and set aside.

Melt half the butter in a frying pan set over a high heat, add the bacon and fry until it starts to crisp. Add the livers and mushrooms and sauté for 1 minute.

Pour over the wine and cream and stir all the ingredients together for 2–3 minutes, but no more, to ensure the livers stay pink in the middle, then remove the pan from the heat.

Add the parsley and season with salt and pepper. Serve with slices of toast, plain or buttered with the remaining butter.

Rack of lamb
with vegetable broth

Serves 4

**20g (¾oz) shelled
   hazelnuts**
**4 large, floury
   potatoes, peeled
   and quartered**
**4 racks of French-
   trimmed lamb (ask
   your butcher to
   prepare these)**
1 tbsp olive oil
**12 baby onions, peeled
   but left whole**
**800ml (29fl oz) beef
   stock**
200g (7oz) broad beans
**250g (9oz) asparagus
   tips**
**110g (4oz) French
   beans, topped and
   tailed**
40g (1½oz) butter
**110ml (4fl oz) double
   cream**
**2 tbsp chopped flat-
   leaf parsley**
**4 tsp hazelnut oil
   (optional)**
Salt and black pepper

*My favourite lamb supplier is Colin Robinson, a family butcher
from Skipton, North Yorkshire. If you're in the area, pay him a
visit. I promise you won't be disappointed.*

Preheat the oven to 200°C (400°F), Gas 6. Roast the hazelnuts
on a baking tray for 15–20 minutes, or until the skins split.
Take out of the oven, tip into a clean tea towel and rub to
remove the skins. Once cooled, chop the nuts in half.

Place the potatoes and a good pinch of salt in a large saucepan
of water. Bring to the boil and cook for 20–25 minutes.

Season the lamb with salt and pepper. Put the olive oil in a
roasting tin, place over a high heat and add the lamb. Seal on
all sides, especially the side with the fat. Add the onions to the
tin and put in the oven for 6 minutes. Remove from the oven,
add the hazelnuts and return to the oven for 6 minutes more.

Pour the stock into another large saucepan, bring to the boil
and reduce by half. Add the broad beans, cook for 3–4
minutes, then remove them (reserving the stock) and refresh
in cold water. Peel off the skins. Just before the lamb is ready,
add the asparagus tips and French beans to the stock to cook.
Remove the lamb from the oven and allow to rest in the tin.
Meanwhile, drain the potatoes, return to the pan and mash
with butter and cream. Add salt and pepper and keep warm.

Drain the fat from the lamb and add the hazelnuts and onions
to the stock. Return the peeled broad beans, add the parsley,
and season with salt and pepper. Slice each rack of lamb in
half and place with the mash in the centre of bowls. Spoon the
broth around and drizzle with hazelnut oil, if you wish.

Lamb, mint and Little Gem salad

Serves 4

2 racks of lamb, bones removed (ask your butcher to do this)
1 tbsp olive oil
3 sprigs of rosemary
50g (2oz) butter, cut into cubes
2 Little Gem lettuces
Salt and black pepper

For the dressing
1 tsp caster sugar
25ml (1fl oz) Chardonnay vinegar or other white wine vinegar
75ml (3fl oz) extra-virgin olive oil
1 tbsp chopped mint
Salt and black pepper

This simple and delicious salad can be eaten hot, warm or even cold, whichever way you prefer. It reminds me of my gran – like me, she loved fresh mint in salads or eaten with lamb. So, Gran, this recipe is in memory of you.

Preheat the oven to 200°C (400°F), Gas 6.

Trim the lamb, removing excess fat if you wish, and, using a piece of string, tie up into a tight roll. Season with salt and pepper.

Set an ovenproof pan or roasting tin over a high heat, add the tablespoon of olive oil and then the lamb, turning it in the pan for 2–3 minutes to seal on all sides, so that it is an even golden colour. Add the rosemary and the butter and remove the pan from the heat.

Roast in the oven for 8 minutes, basting from time to time with the butter, then remove from the oven. When the lamb has cooled slightly, remove from the pan, wrap in cling film tightly with the rosemary and set aside on a chopping board.

Place the sugar and the vinegar in a bowl, mix well then add the extra-virgin olive oil and the mint. Season with salt and pepper, to taste, stir together and pour into a serving jug.

Place the leaves from the lettuces in a serving bowl. Remove the lamb from the cling film, slice very thinly and serve with the salad leaves and the jug of dressing on the side.

Côte de boeuf with watercress and black beer mustard

Makes 2 large portions or 4 smaller ones

1kg (2lb 2oz) rib of beef with the chine bone removed (ask your butcher to do this for you)
2 tbsp olive oil
Salt and black pepper
110g (4oz) Black Beer Mustard (see page 36), to serve

For the watercress salad
1 tbsp cider vinegar
3 tbsp rapeseed or extra-virgin olive oil
1 tsp Black Beer Mustard (see page 36)
110–150g (4–5oz) watercress, thick stalks removed
Salt and black pepper

Côte de boeuf is a large cut of beef with a big, thick rib bone. If you can't get it, use a thick rib-eye steak instead. This is equally delicious cooked on a barbecue in summer for 10–15 minutes on each side.

Season the beef with salt and pepper and brush with the olive oil. Set a frying pan over a high heat and, when it starts to smoke, add the beef and cook for 4–5 minutes on one side, then turn over and cook for a further 4–5 minutes. Turn the beef to seal the edges and cook for a further 4 minutes on each side, or 8–10 minutes per side if you prefer your meat well done.

Remove the beef from the pan, place on a chopping board and allow to rest for 5 minutes before carving.

To make the watercress salad, whisk the vinegar, rapeseed or olive oil and mustard together in a bowl and season to taste with salt and pepper. Place the watercress in another bowl and drizzle over the dressing, tossing the leaves to coat evenly. Place in a serving bowl and set aside.

To serve, cut the beef into fairly thick slices and serve the mustard and the watercress on the side.

Black beer mustard

Makes 425g (15oz)
Vegetarian

25g (1oz) white
   mustard seeds
110g (4oz) black
   mustard seeds
75g (3oz) light soft
   brown sugar
1 tsp allspice berries
1 tsp paprika
½ tsp turmeric
2 tsp sea salt
1 tsp crushed black
   peppercorns
175ml (6fl oz) red wine
   vinegar
40ml (1½fl oz) balsamic
   vinegar
3 tbsp runny honey
110ml (4fl oz) bottled
   Black Sheep Ale or
   other traditionally-
   made British beer

Mustard is very easy to make and handy to keep in your store cupboard. It goes well with many types of meat – try it with the Yorkshire ham on page 39.

Put all the dry ingredients into a food processor or blender and blend until the seeds are roughly crushed. Transfer to a bowl and stir in the two vinegars, honey and ale.

Cover the mustard with cling film and place in the fridge for 2 hours. If you want to keep the mustard longer, put into sterilised jars (see page 166) and store in a cool, dark place. The mustard should then keep for 3–6 months.

Juniper-pickled cucumbers

Makes 400g (14oz)
Vegetarian

250ml (9fl oz) pickling
    malt vinegar
1 tsp juniper berries
125g (4½oz) caster sugar
1 tbsp olive oil
1 tbsp mustard seeds
2 large cucumbers,
    deseeded and cut into
    2cm (¾in) cubes
Salt and black pepper

This will keep for 3–4 days in the fridge if stored in sealed, sterilised jars (see page 166). The pickle can be seen in the picture on page 47.

Place the vinegar, juniper berries and sugar in a small saucepan and bring to the boil. Remove from the heat. Pour the olive oil into a frying pan set over a medium–high heat, add the mustard seeds and cook until the seeds start to pop.

Add the cucumber and fry for 2–3 minutes. Season, to taste, with salt and pepper. Place in a bowl, pour over the vinegar mixture and stir well. Allow to cool completely, then place in the fridge.

Sliced Yorkshire ham with poached leeks and spring onions

Serves 4

6 black peppercorns
Pinch of salt
1 bay leaf
1 medium leek,
trimmed and outer
leaves removed
8 spring onions
400g (14oz) York or
any other roast ham,
ready-sliced if you
prefer
Chervil leaves, to
garnish

For the glaze
4 tbsp English mustard
2 tbsp runny honey
150ml (6fl oz) rapeseed
or extra-virgin olive
oil
Zest of 2 oranges
4 tbsp white wine
vinegar
Salt and black pepper

Until recently, one of the few places you could buy a real 'York ham' was Scott's butchers in York, but sadly, after 150 years of trading, it is now closed. Despite this, the UK still produces the best pork in the world and we should make the most of it. This recipe is best served warm; however, if you choose to serve it cold, make just half the quantity of the glaze to drizzle over the ham in the final step.

Half fill a large saucepan with water, add the peppercorns, salt and bay leaf and bring to the boil. Once the water is boiling, add the leek whole (if it doesn't fit, cut in half widthways). Reduce the heat and cook for 6–8 minutes on a gentle simmer. Add the spring onions and cook for a further 3 minutes, then drain the vegetables and allow to cool.

To make the glaze, place the mustard and honey in a bowl, slowly whisk in the rapeseed or olive oil, then add the orange zest and vinegar, season with salt and pepper and set aside.

If you wish to warm the meat, place the whole ham or the slices on a baking tray and spoon half of the glaze over the top. Put in a preheated oven at 170°C (325°F), Gas 3, for 1 hour if the ham is whole or, if it is ready-sliced, until heated through. Remove from the oven and, if necessary, carve the ham into slices.

Place the sliced ham on a board or platter, then slice the leek into 1cm (½in) rounds and the spring onion into bite-sized lengths. Arrange these on the ham, drizzle with the rest of the glaze, place a few chervil leaves on top and serve.

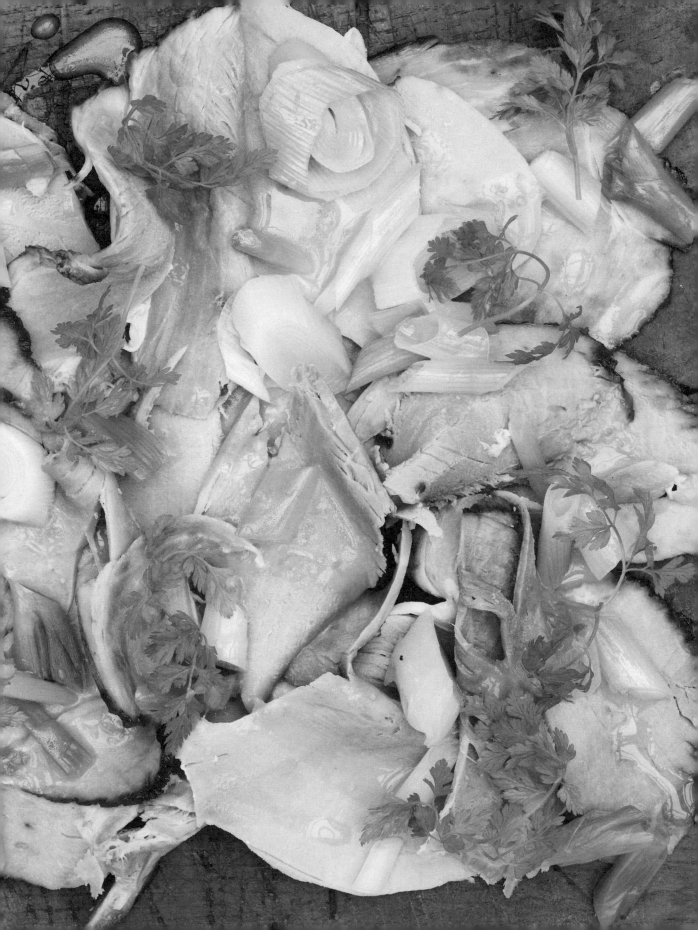

Scotch eggs with curried salad cream

Serves 4

**8 small eggs and
4 medium eggs
(reserve 2 for the
salad cream)**
**450g (1lb) good-
quality pork
sausages or
sausagemeat**
**300g (11oz) dried
breadcrumbs, such
as Japanese panko**
**1.2 litres (2 pints)
vegetable oil, for
deep-frying**

For the salad cream
**2 hard-boiled egg yolks
(see above)**
2 tsp English mustard
**150ml (5fl oz) rapeseed
oil or extra-virgin
olive oil**
**1 tbsp white wine
vinegar**
**75 ml (3fl oz) double
cream**
**1 tbsp mild curry
powder, or to taste**
Salt and black pepper

*We're all kids at heart, so who wouldn't love these delicious eggs?
The curried salad cream adds a nice spicy touch and will keep for
two days in the fridge, although it's best used fresh.*

Fill a large saucepan with water and bring to the boil. Place
the eight small eggs and two of the medium eggs in the
boiling water. Remove the eight small eggs after 2–3 minutes
and the two medium eggs after 7–8 minutes. Run under
cold water immediately to stop them cooking any further,
then peel them whole, and set the two medium ones aside.

Remove the skin from the sausages (if using), then dip your
hands in cold water and divide the meat into eight balls.
With wet hands, press the centre of each ball to make a well.
Place a small cooked egg in each well and carefully close the
meat around it. Place them on a large plate in the fridge and
leave for about 2 hours to firm up.

Place the two uncooked eggs in a shallow bowl and whisk
with a fork. Pour the breadcrumbs onto a plate. Dip each
Scotch egg in the whisked egg, then roll in the crumbs and
return to the fridge for 30 minutes. Repeat the process until
each egg has a double layer of crumbs.

Meanwhile, make the salad cream. Push the yolks from the
two hard-boiled medium eggs through a sieve into a bowl,
then beat in the mustard, season with salt and pepper and
place in a blender or food processor. Alternatively, use a
hand-held beater for whisking the ingredients together.

Continued overleaf …

Whisk in the rapeseed or olive oil while the machine is on, pouring in a few drops at a time. When smoothly amalgamated, whisk in the vinegar, again a little at a time, and then slowly add the cream. Add the curry powder and season with more salt and pepper, to taste, if needed.

If using a deep-fat fryer, heat the vegetable oil to 150°C (300°F) – not too hot or the eggs will explode and the meat will not cook through. Alternatively, fill a deep, heavy-based frying pan to a depth of 2cm (¾in) with oil and use a sugar thermometer to check that it has reached the correct temperature. Carefully lower the Scotch eggs into the oil and cook for 5–7 minutes.

When cooked, serve hot or cold, with salad cream on the side.

Pressed ham terrine

Serves 4

1.5kg (3lb 4oz) ham hocks
1 onion, peeled and roughly chopped
½ tsp black peppercorns
1 tsp salt
2 sprigs of rosemary
2 bay leaves
3 leaves of gelatine
6 tbsp chopped flat-leaf parsley
Extra salt and black pepper
Crusty bread, to serve

From the base of a pig's leg bone, a ham hock is an inexpensive cut of meat that is often overlooked. There isn't loads of meat on it, so you'll need several for this recipe. Serve with cucumber pickle (see page 37) and a pile of crusty bread or warm boiled potatoes.

Place the ham hocks in a large, deep saucepan, along with the onion, peppercorns, salt, rosemary and bay leaves. Cover with water and bring to the boil, then reduce the heat and simmer for 2 hours. Remove from the heat and allow to cool in the pan.

Take the hocks from the pan and set aside. Strain the cooking liquid through a fine sieve and pour 250ml (9fl oz) of it into a saucepan set over a medium heat. Place the gelatine leaves in a bowl of cold water and soak for 5 minutes until pliable, then drain the water off and add the gelatine to the hot liquid. Stir well and allow to cool.

Remove the ham from the bones and cut into 2.5cm (1in) pieces, tearing if needed. Mix with the parsley and season lightly with salt and pepper. Line a glass bowl or terrine dish about 1.2 litres (2 pints) in size with a large piece of cling film and spread a quarter of the ham pieces over the base.

Spoon over some of the gelatine liquid, add another quarter of the ham and more gelatine, repeating for two further layers and pouring over the remaining gelatine with the final layer. Stretch cling film loosely over the top, then a layer of foil, and place in the fridge – on a plate, to catch any drips – for 2 hours with a weight or weights pressing on the top.

To serve, take the terrine from the fridge, remove the cling film and accompany with pickled cucumber and crusty bread.

Rhubarb and ginger syllabub

Serves 4

2 sticks of rhubarb (preferably forced variety), cut into 1cm (½in) cubes
2.5cm (1in) piece of root ginger, peeled and chopped
4 tbsp caster sugar
50ml (2fl oz) white wine
75g (3oz) mascarpone
250ml (9fl oz) double cream
2–4 tbsp icing sugar
1 piece of crystallised ginger, finely chopped

I wouldn't be allowed back over the Yorkshire border if I didn't put some rhubarb recipes in this book. Yorkshire is famous for parkin and puddings, but above all else, it's celebrated for its rhubarb. The famous 'rhubarb triangle' is an area of land between Leeds, Wakefield and Bradford. This is where most of Britain's forced rhubarb comes from.

Place the rhubarb, root ginger and sugar in a medium-sized saucepan and add the white wine. Set over a low–medium heat and bring to a simmer, not allowing it to boil. Cook for 4–5 minutes, or until the rhubarb is softened, then remove from the heat and set aside.

When the mixture has cooled, remove 2 tablespoonfuls to a separate bowl and mash with a fork. In another bowl, whip the mascarpone and cream together with the icing sugar and when the mixture forms soft peaks, fold in the mashed rhubarb and ginger mixture.

Spoon the rest of the poached rhubarb into bowls or glasses, then spoon over the mascarpone mixture and sprinkle the crystallised ginger over the top.

Orange cheesecake with roasted rhubarb

Serves 4

450g (1lb) full fat cream cheese
Zest and juice of 4 oranges (zest and juice kept separate)
250g (9oz) caster sugar
400ml (14fl oz) double cream
250g (9oz) crème fraîche
200g (7oz) forced rhubarb, or tender pink stems from the garden, cut into 5cm (2in) lengths
50g (2oz) butter, cut into cubes
4 shortbread biscuits

I've tried many cheesecake recipes over the years, but this is my favourite. It can be made with different flavours, too, such as vanilla, chocolate, strawberry or raspberry. The cakes look best when made in professional chef's rings, which can be bought from a good cookshop or over the internet.

To make the cheesecake filling, place the cream cheese in a bowl and combine with the orange zest and 200g (7oz) of the sugar, then in another bowl whip up the double cream until it forms soft peaks.

Carefully fold together the whipped cream, the cream cheese mixture and the crème fraîche – don't over-mix or the mixture will split. Then spoon into 6cm (2½in) chef's rings and place on a baking tray in the fridge for 2 hours to firm up.

Preheat the oven to 240°C (475F), Gas 9. Put the rhubarb in an ovenproof dish, cover with the remaining sugar, the butter and the orange juice, and place in the oven for 8–10 minutes. Cooking in a very hot oven should cause the juice to turn to a nice syrup, but don't overcook as rhubarb turns to mush very quickly. Check to see if it is cooked by squeezing one of the pieces, then remove and allow to cool to room temperature.

To serve, crush the shortbread to fine crumbs and remove the cheesecakes from the fridge. Roll the top and bottom of each cake in the biscuit crumbs and place on a plate. Then, using either a warm tea towel or a cook's blowtorch, warm the rings slightly and they should just lift off. Serve with the rhubarb on the side and drizzle with some of the juices from the dish.

Crème caramel with strawberries

Serves 4–6

150ml (5fl oz) milk
300ml (11fl oz) double cream
1 vanilla pod, cut in half
4 large eggs
40g (1½oz) caster sugar
400g (14oz) fresh strawberries, hulled

For the caramel
110g (4oz) caster sugar
2 tbsp hot water

Every nation has its own version of crème caramel, using different types of milk and cream. It keeps well in the fridge, so can be made well ahead of time. Although strawberries are recognised as a summer fruit, they do start coming into season at the very end of spring. If you're making this dessert any earlier in the year, however, you could substitute with poached forced rhubarb.

First make the caramel. Put the sugar in a medium-sized saucepan set over a medium heat. When the sugar begins to melt and darken, stir from time to time and continue to cook until it becomes a uniform syrup and a deep caramel colour.

Take the pan off the heat and carefully add the 2 tablespoons of hot water – it will spit quite a bit at first but will soon settle. Stir for 3–4 minutes and once the water is combined, quickly pour into the bottom of 4–6 x 250ml (9fl oz) ramekins, tipping it around to coat the sides of each dish.

Preheat the oven to 150°C (300°F), Gas 2. Pour the milk and cream into another saucepan, along with the vanilla pod and scraped-out seeds. Set the pan over a low heat and allow the milk and cream to heat up gently while you whisk together the eggs and sugar in a large bowl.

When the milk and cream are steaming hot, but not boiling, pour onto the egg and sugar mixture, whisking well. Pass though a sieve, then pour the liquid into the ramekins and place them in a large roasting tin. Transfer the tin carefully to the oven, then pour enough hot water into the base of the tin to surround the ramekins up to two-thirds in depth. Bake for 1 hour.

Remove the roasting tin from the oven and allow to cool. Chill the crème caramels in the fridge and remove 1 hour before you are ready to serve. Loosen the edges by running a knife around the inside of each ramekin before inverting it on to a plate and serving with fresh strawberries scattered around.

Pancakes with pistachio gremolata

Serves 4
(Makes 8–10 pancakes)

**125g (4½oz) plain
flour**
2 good pinches of salt
2 medium eggs
1 tbsp butter, melted
300ml (11fl oz) milk
**Sunflower oil, for
frying**

For the gremolata
**110g (4oz) butter at
room temperature**
**4 tbsp chopped
pistachios**
4 basil leaves, chopped
**Zest of 2 lemons and
juice of 1 (kept
separate)**
8 tbsp granulated sugar

When cooking a large batch of pancakes, it can be hard to keep them all warm. So why not make in advance and freeze them? Layer between greaseproof paper to prevent them sticking together, then take a few from the freezer whenever you want them and fry briefly or pop under a grill to warm through. Problem solved!

To make the gremolata, place the butter, pistachios, basil and lemon zest in a bowl, add half the sugar and mix well with the juice from just 1 lemon (not too much or it will cause the butter to separate). Then, using your hands, mould into 2cm (¾in) balls and roll in the remaining sugar. Put on a plate and place in the fridge. (The mixture will keep for up to 1 day.)

To make the pancakes, place the flour and salt in a food processor, or use a large bowl and an electric beater, and add the eggs, butter and half the milk. Whiz until smooth and creamy, scraping the sides of the bowl occasionally to dislodge any lumps or stray pockets of flour. With the motor running, mix in the remaining milk.

Set a frying pan over a medium–high heat, drizzle with sunflower oil then pour in a thin layer of batter. Allow to cook for 1 minute, then flip over and cook for a further minute. Remove from the pan and place between sheets of greaseproof paper on a warmed serving plate (or in the oven, set low – for no longer than 10 minutes or they will dry out). Repeat the process until all the mix has been used.

To serve, remove the gremolata from the fridge and place a ball on top of each pancake.

Baked Alaska with elderflower meringue

Serves 4–6

1 x 15cm (6in) disc of plain sponge

1–2 tbsp freshly squeezed orange juice

2–3 tbsp strawberry jam

500ml (18fl oz) vanilla ice cream

For the elderflower meringue

225g (8oz) caster sugar

30g (1¼oz) glucose (optional)

4 egg whites

6 elderflower heads, flowers stripped from stalks

For the berry sauce (optional)

200g (7oz) frozen mixed berries, defrosted

2 tbsp icing sugar

This retro dessert from the '60s and '70s became a favourite of mine while I was working in France almost twenty years ago. Unless you have some leftover sponge cake lurking in a tin, simply use a bought sponge for the base – either the bottom half of a Victoria sponge (jam included, though you may want to add more) or patched-together trifle sponges, cut to shape.

First make the elderflower meringue. Pour 90ml (3½fl oz) water into a medium-sized saucepan, then add the sugar and glucose, if using. Set over a moderate heat and stir the mixture until it boils. Skim the surface with a spoon to remove any sugar crystals and brush down any crystals that form on the sides of the pan with a brush dipped in cold water. Now increase the heat so that the syrup cooks rapidly.

Insert a sugar thermometer to check the temperature. When the sugar reaches 110°C (225°F), whisk the egg whites in a food processor until they form stiff peaks. Take the sugar off the heat when it reaches 120°C (250°F).

When the egg whites are well risen and firm, set the food processor to the lowest speed and gently pour on the sugar syrup in a thin stream, taking care not to let it run on to the whisks. Continue to beat at low speed until the mixture is almost completely cold; this will take about 15 minutes. Then add the elderflowers. The meringue is now ready to use.

Continued overleaf ...

Preheat the oven to 200°C (400°F), Gas 6. To assemble the Alaska, place the disc of sponge on a plate and drizzle with the orange juice. Spread thickly with strawberry jam and spoon the ice cream on top, smoothing the surface to form an even mound.

Spread most of the elderflower meringue over the ice cream, using a palette knife to seal in the ingredients. Place the remainder of the meringue in a piping bag with a star nozzle and pipe around the edge and on the top, or use a spoon and palette knife to shape the meringue.

Put the Alaska on to a baking sheet, then place in the oven and cook for 2 minutes, or until the edges of the Alaska turn golden brown. Alternatively, quickly go around the edge with a cook's blowtorch to colour the meringue.

To make the berry sauce (if using), blend the berries, icing sugar and 25ml (1fl oz) water together using a hand-held blender, then pass through a sieve. Drizzle the Alaska with the sauce or serve it just as it is.

Elderflower fritters with maple syrup

Serves 4

1.2 litres (2 pints) vegetable oil, for deep-frying

2 eggs, separated into whites and yolks

200ml (7fl oz) milk

110g (4oz) plain flour

10–12 elderflower heads, cut into small florets

25g (1oz) caster sugar

150ml (5fl oz) maple syrup

Elderflowers make the best fritters and this is one of the quickest puddings to prepare. For the fritters to be nice and crisp, the oil for frying them must be so hot that they fizz when you drop them in. Cook them in batches and keep the cooked fritters warm while you finish the rest.

If using a deep-fat fryer, heat the vegetable oil to 180°C (350°F). Alternatively, fill a deep, heavy-based frying pan to a depth of 2cm (¾in) with oil and use a sugar thermometer to check that it has reached the correct temperature.

Place the egg whites in one bowl and the egg yolks in another. Whisk the whites until they form soft peaks, then set aside.

Add the milk and flour to the bowl with the yolks and mix well. When combined, gently fold in the whisked egg whites. Don't be too vigorous or you will lose all of the air.

Dip each of the elderflower florets into the batter mix and place in the fryer or the pan. Fry until golden brown, then remove with a slotted spoon and drain on kitchen paper. Sprinkle with caster sugar.

Gently warm the maple syrup in a small saucepan, then remove from the heat and pour into a serving bowl. Serve alongside the elderflower fritters for dipping.

Elderflower and lemon cordial

Makes 2 litres
(3½ pints)

24 elderflower heads
1.8kg (4lb) caster sugar
2 unwaxed lemons
75g (3oz) citric acid

When I was growing up, I couldn't wait for the elderflower season. It was a great excuse to run around the garden whacking my sister with a whippy branch of blossom. It also meant there was an alternative drink to barley water, which I hated. Elderflower cordial made a refreshing change and still does!

Shake the elderflowers over the sink to get rid of any insects, and then place in a large bowl. Put the sugar into a large saucepan with 1.2 litres (2 pints) water and bring to the boil, stirring until the sugar has dissolved.

While the sugar syrup is heating, peel the zest off the lemons in wide strips with a potato peeler and toss into the bowl with the elderflowers. Slice the lemons and add to the bowl.

Pour over the boiling sugar syrup, and then stir in the citric acid. Cover with a clean tea towel and then leave out at room temperature for 24 hours.

After 24 hours, strain the cordial through a sieve or a colander lined with muslin or a clean tea towel, and pour into thoroughly cleaned glass or plastic bottles. Screw on the lids and place somewhere cool. It keeps for 2–3 weeks.

To serve, dilute the cordial with some fizzy water and add slices of freshly cut lemon and some ice cubes.

Summer

Tomatoes • Cucumbers • Chard • Salad leaves
Fennel • Sweetcorn • Broad beans • Cherries
Redcurrants • Strawberries • Sardines • Crab

At this time of year, different fruit and vegetables come and go quite quickly, but there is no better time to enjoy an abundance of fresh, delicious, British food. Cherries dangle from the trees and redcurrants fill the bushes, while the strawberry beds are crammed with fruit. There are fresh salad leaves, full of flavour, and my greenhouse bursts with tomatoes, peppers and chillies. There are beans and peas, too, twisting round their canes, and all are ready to be picked.

Pea soup with Little Gem and marjoram

Serves 4–6

2 tbsp chopped marjoram

500g (1lb 2oz) fresh or frozen peas (shelled weight)

2 tbsp extra-virgin olive oil, plus extra for drizzling (optional)

150ml (5fl oz) double cream

2 Little Gem lettuces, cut in half

4 slices of Parma ham (optional)

Salt and black pepper

This fresh, green soup is an excellent use for the summer crop of garden peas. Marjoram is easy to grow in the garden or in a pot. It's a hardy herb, so you can plant it in the winter months ready for the spring. If you can't find it, use oregano instead. For an entirely vegetarian version of this soup, simply leave out the Parma ham.

Bring 1 litre (1¾ pints) water to the boil in a large saucepan and add a big pinch of salt. Tip in the marjoram and peas, bring the liquid back up to the boil and cook for 2–3 minutes, or until the peas are just tender and still bright green.

Strain the marjoram and peas, retaining the cooking liquid, and transfer the peas to a food processor or blender. Add just enough of the cooking liquid to cover the peas, then blend for a couple of minutes, to create a smooth purée.

Season, to taste, with salt and pepper and add 1 tablespoon of the olive oil and the cream. Pulse in the food processor for a few seconds, then place in a saucepan, set over a low heat, to keep warm.

Set a frying pan over a medium heat, add another tablespoon of the oil and fry the lettuce and ham on both sides for 2–3 minutes in total.

To serve, divide the soup between warmed bowls, place a lettuce half in the centre of each, sprinkle with pieces of ham and drizzle with the remaining olive oil, if you wish.

Sweetcorn soup with crab and basil cream

Serves 4–6

25g (1oz) butter
1 onion, peeled and chopped
225g (8oz) potatoes, peeled and cut into cubes
1 tbsp medium curry powder (optional)
575g (1lb 5oz) tinned sweetcorn kernels (drained weight)
150ml (5fl oz) double cream
250g (9oz) mixed crab meat, white and dark
1 tbsp extra-virgin olive oil, for drizzling
Salt and black pepper

For the basil cream
5g (¼oz) basil leaves
50ml (2fl oz) double cream

When I was working out in Singapore I discovered two great dishes. One was their famous chilli crab and the other was a soup very similar to this. I liked it so much I turned it into a recipe you can make at home. Use the brown crab meat as well as the white, as it contains most of the flavour.

Place the basil in a blender and purée until finely chopped, then add the double cream and mix until thick. Put in the fridge to chill.

Melt the butter in a large saucepan set over a medium heat. Add the onion, potatoes and curry powder (if using) and cook until the vegetables are soft but not browned.

Pour in 1 litre (1¾ pints) water, season with salt and pepper, and stir the ingredients together. Bring to the boil, then reduce the heat and simmer for 6–7 minutes, or until the potatoes are just tender.

Add the sweetcorn kernels to the soup and simmer for 3 minutes. Remove from the heat and pour into a blender or food processor, add the double cream, blitz to a purée and return to the pan. Simmer for a further 3 minutes. Add the crab meat and mix well together.

To serve, ladle the hot soup into bowls, add a spoonful of the chilled basil cream on top of each, plus a drizzle of olive oil.

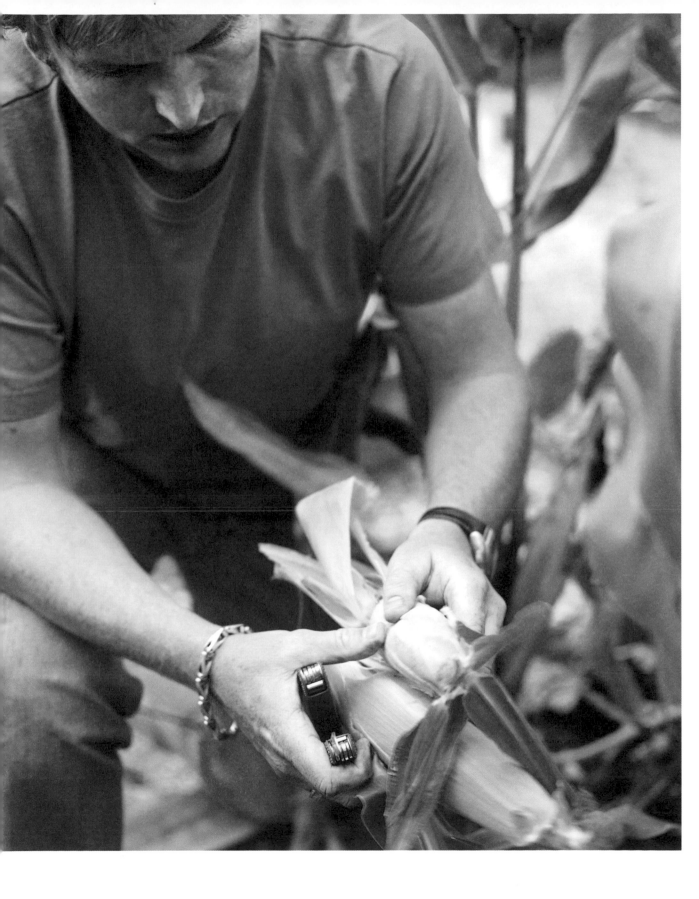

Deep-fried tomato fritters with red onion salad

Serves 4–5
Vegetarian

**1.2 litres (2 pints)
vegetable oil, for
deep-frying**
4 tsp rice vinegar
2 tsp caster sugar
**2 red onions, peeled
and thinly sliced**
**2 beef tomatoes, very
finely sliced
widthways**
1 tsp capers
**15g (½oz) flat-leaf
parsley, leaves only**
**2 tbsp extra-virgin
olive oil**

For the tempura batter
25g (1oz) plain flour
25g (1oz) cornflour
**50–75ml (2–3fl oz)
sparkling mineral
water, chilled**
Salt and black pepper

These tomatoes make a great starter but they need to be fried right at the last minute or they will go soggy. The firmer the tomatoes, the easier they are to use as they will keep their shape better.

If using a deep-fat fryer, heat the vegetable oil to 180°C (350°F). Alternatively, fill a deep, heavy-based frying pan to a depth of 2cm (¾in) with oil and use a sugar thermometer to check that it has reached the correct temperature.

To make the salad, first warm the vinegar and sugar in a small saucepan and stir until the sugar has dissolved. Place the onions in a bowl, pour over the warmed vinegar mixture and cover with cling film. Allow to cool completely, stirring occasionally.

Meanwhile, make the tempura batter. Put the flour and cornflour in a bowl and gradually add the water until it just starts to thicken, then season with salt and pepper. Take the sliced tomatoes and dip them into the batter mix.

Drop the tomatoes into the deep-fat fryer or frying pan and allow to cook for 3–4 minutes or until golden brown, then carefully remove with a slotted spoon and drain thoroughly on kitchen paper.

Add the capers, parsley and olive oil to the onions and mix together, seasoning with salt and pepper, to taste. Spoon on to plates, top with the tomato fritters and serve.

Tomato, basil and mozzarella pizzas

Makes 4 pizzas
Vegetarian

For the pizza base
500g (1lb 2oz) strong white flour, plus extra, for dusting
1 tsp salt
1 tsp caster sugar
8g (⅓oz) dried or 5g (¼oz) fresh yeast
300ml (11fl oz) still mineral water

For the topping
2 bunches of basil, leaves only
50ml (2fl oz) extra-virgin olive oil, plus extra, for drizzling
1 small onion, peeled and finely chopped
2 cloves of garlic, peeled and chopped
2 x 400g cans of chopped tomatoes
1 tsp caster sugar
350g (12oz) buffalo mozzarella, in pieces
110g (4oz) Parmesan cheese, freshly grated
Salt and black pepper

I built a pizza oven in my garden a few years ago. The first few times I used it, the roof caught fire and I had to rebuild it … those were some expensive pizzas! Now it works brilliantly and the pizzas taste fantastic, although you can make them in a regular oven just as well.

To make the pizza base, place the flour, salt and sugar in a large mixing bowl. In another, smaller, bowl, mix the yeast with 50ml (2fl oz) mineral water. Pour the yeast mixture into the centre of the flour, add the remaining water and mix to form a soft dough.

Put the dough on a floured work surface and knead until smooth and elastic. This should take at least 5 minutes, as the dough requires a proper kneading to achieve the right texture for the pizza bases. Once kneaded, place the dough in a clean, greased mixing bowl, cover with cling film or a clean tea towel and leave to rise for 1 hour.

While the dough is rising, make the pizza topping. Chop half of the basil leaves and set the rest aside. Put a frying pan over a medium–high heat, then add the olive oil, onion and garlic and fry for 2 minutes.

Add the tomatoes, sugar and chopped basil to the frying pan, bring to a simmer and cook for 30 minutes, or until the sauce has thickened. Season with salt and pepper and leave to cool.

Continued overleaf…

Remove the dough from the bowl and knead for 1 minute on a floured work surface, then divide into four pieces and roll into circles, each 0.5cm (¼in) thick. If you're a bit of a pizza expert, then spin each base into shape by whirling it around your head, but I'm not, so I use a rolling pin!

Preheat the oven to 220°C (425°F), Gas 7 and place a heavy baking sheet or a pizza stone in the oven to warm up. Place the pizza bases on another, heavily floured, baking sheet. Spread the cooled tomato sauce thinly over the pizzas and top with the mozzarella and Parmesan.

Quickly slide the pizzas into the oven, pushing them from the floured sheet onto the hot pizza stone or baking sheet, and cook for 10 minutes, or longer, epending on how thick the bases are. When cooked, remove from the oven and serve, sprinkled with the whole basil leaves and more olive oil. Of course, you can make these pizzas with many other toppings – just follow the method for the bases and change the toppings as you wish.

Slow-roasted tomatoes with Worcestershire sauce

Serves 4

12 English tomatoes, cut in half
1 x 295ml bottle of Worcestershire sauce
8 tbsp rapeseed or extra-virgin olive oil
1 tbsp English mustard powder
Celery salt and black pepper

This is a very English breakfast or brunch. Don't worry if it initially looks like there's too much sauce – it will evaporate as it cooks. These tomatoes can be served hot or cold, or as a side dish for a barbecue (see picture on page 85). For a vegetarian version of this dish, substitute the Worcestershire sauce for a variety without anchovies.

Preheat the oven to 230°C (450°F), Gas 8.

Place the tomatoes, cut side up, on a baking tray, and drizzle the whole bottle of Worcestershire sauce over the top. Drizzle over the rapeseed or olive oil and sprinkle with black pepper and the mustard powder.

Place in the oven and cook for 12–15 minutes until soft. During cooking, remove the tomatoes from the oven every 4 minutes to baste with the juices from the tray.

When cooked, remove the tomatoes from the oven, sprinkle with celery salt and place on individual plates to serve.

Soused herrings with red chilli and chive cream

Serves 6

6 herrings, filleted and
    pin bones removed
    (your fishmonger
    can do this)
250ml (9fl oz) malt
    vinegar
3 shallots, peeled and
    chopped
1 red chilli, deseeded
    and finely sliced
1 large bay leaf
½ tsp fennel seeds
½ tsp cumin seeds
¼ tsp black
    peppercorns
½ tsp sea salt
Zest and juice of
    1 lemon
2 cloves of garlic,
    peeled and chopped

For the chive cream
110ml (4fl oz) double
    cream
25g (1oz) chives,
    chopped

On a visit to the Isle of Bute, I was able to see for myself how the UK fishing industry has declined. I was told that, back in the 1860s, over 500 fishing boats used to land at the island to unload herrings. Now, only a handful are left. It's a shame, because herrings make a fantastic, simple meal, whether soused, turned into kippers, or just popped under the grill.

Preheat the oven to 180°C (350°F), Gas 4.

To make the chive cream, pour the cream into a bowl and whip until it forms soft peaks. Add the chives and mix thoroughly together, then place in the fridge while you cook the herrings.

Place the herring fillets, skin side down, on a chopping board and roll each fillet up from the head to the tail. Secure with a cocktail stick and arrange in an ovenproof dish.

Put all the other ingredients into a medium-sized saucepan together with 125ml (4½fl oz) water and gently warm over a low heat for 4–5 minutes, then pour the sauce over the herring fillets and cover the dish with foil. Bake in the oven for 20 minutes.

Remove from the oven and allow to cool. Serve straight away, with a dollop of the chive cream per portion. Alternatively, place the fish in an air-tight container or Kilner jar and pour in enough of the liquid to cover. Pickle the fish in the fridge for 6–8 days and eat cold.

Smoked haddock, globe artichoke and lemon risotto

Serves 4

25g (1oz) butter
½ small onion, peeled and chopped
300g (11oz) Arborio rice
110ml (4fl oz) white wine
1 litre (1¾ pints) Fish Stock (see page 217)
400ml (14fl oz) milk
250g (9oz) natural smoked haddock
4 small globe artichokes, outer leaves removed
3 tbsp chopped flat-leaf parsley
Zest and juice of 2 lemons
2 tbsp mascarpone
110g (4oz) Parmesan cheese, freshly grated
Salt and black pepper

My Italian mates will moan and groan at this one – putting fish in a risotto is a no-no, apparently! But just taste it. The ingredients go together brilliantly and it's one of the most popular dishes on my bistro menu.

Set a large, heavy-based saucepan over a medium heat, and add the butter and onion. Soften for 2 minutes without letting it brown, then add the rice and the wine. Bring to the boil and add the stock little by little, simmering gently for 13–14 minutes and stirring frequently to prevent the rice from sticking to the base of the pan. Test whether it is cooked by tasting it or by squeezing it between your fingers.

While the rice is cooking, pour the milk into another saucepan, add the haddock and bring to the boil. Simmer for 3 minutes and then remove from the heat.

Remove the haddock from the pan, retaining the milk, and flake the fish on to a plate, then set aside. Thinly slice the globe artichokes and place in a bowl with the parsley and half the lemon juice.

Add the lemon zest and remaining juice to the rice. Tip in three-quarters of the flaked haddock and the same quantity of the artichokes, then add the mascarpone and Parmesan. Season with salt and pepper and mix well together. The risotto should be quite runny, so add a little of the poaching milk if it is too thick.

Spoon the risotto into bowls, top with the rest of the haddock and artichokes and serve.

Scallop and squid salad with fennel and rocket

Serves 4

2 small fennel bulbs
**400g (14oz) small
squid**
8 large scallops
**1 tbsp extra-virgin olive
oil**
75g (3oz) rocket
Salt and black pepper

For the dressing
**20g (¾oz) dill,
chopped**
**15g (½oz) parsley,
chopped**
**15g (½oz) coriander,
chopped**
**Zest and juice of
2 limes**
**1 red chilli, deseeded
and chopped**
1 tbsp sumac or allspice
**75ml (3fl oz) extra-
virgin olive oil**

*Hand-dived scallops are worth seeking out, as they are kinder
to the seabed than dredged ones. On a visit to the Isle of Mann,
I met the Croft brothers, who run a business called Island Seafare
(see Supplier list on page 219). Their produce is superb – you can
order amazing scallops and fantastic smoked salmon from their
website. This dish also includes sumac, a citrusy spice commonly
used in Middle Eastern cooking. It can be found in good delis
or bought online.*

Remove the base root from the fennel bulbs and thinly slice
widthways using a sharp knife, then place in a large bowl. In
another bowl, mix together all the ingredients for the dressing
and season with salt and pepper, to taste.

Chop the squid into smaller pieces and put along with the
scallops on to a large plate. Season with salt and pepper and
drizzle with the olive oil. Set a non-stick frying pan over a
high heat and fry the scallops and squid for 3–4 minutes,
turning once. It's best not to cook all the scallops and squid
at once but to fry them in batches to maintain a high level
of heat in the pan.

Put the squid and the scallops in the bowl with the fennel.
Add the rocket, pour over the dressing and toss to coat.
Place on a serving plate and tuck in.

Spicy crab linguini

Serves 4

200g (7oz) linguini
25g (1oz) butter
2 shallots, peeled and
finely chopped
1 garlic clove, peeled
and finely chopped
2 green chillies, finely
chopped
½ tbsp Thai green curry
paste
110 ml (4fl oz) white
wine
200ml (7fl oz) Chicken
Stock (see page 216)
Good pinch of saffron
200ml (7fl oz) double
cream
400g (14oz) mixed crab
meat, white and dark
10g (½oz) flat-leaf
parsley, roughly
chopped
10g (½oz) coriander
leaves, roughly
chopped
Juice of 1 lime
Salt and black pepper

If you want a quick but impressive-looking pasta dish, this is it. Once the ingredients are prepared and the pasta has been cooked, it takes just 5 minutes to make the crab sauce, but looks and tastes as if you spent hours labouring over a hot stove.

Bring a large saucepan of salted water to the boil, add the linguini and cook for 10–12 minutes or according to the instructions on the packet. Drain and set aside.

Melt the butter in a large saucepan set over a medium heat and add the shallots and garlic. Fry for about 1 minute, without browning, then add the chillies and curry paste and cook for 2–3 minutes.

Pour in the wine, bring to the boil and reduce the liquid by half, then add the stock and saffron and simmer for 2–3 minutes. Pour in the cream, bring back up to the boil and remove from the heat.

Add the crab meat to the sauce and heat gently for 2–3 minutes, then add the cooked linguini and warm through, stirring the sauce and pasta together. Remove from the heat, then stir in the parsley, coriander and lime juice, and season with salt and pepper. Serve immediately.

Grilled sardines with panzanella

Serves 4

½ slightly stale
   baguette
2 cloves of garlic,
   peeled
2 plum tomatoes,
   roughly chopped
15g (½oz) basil leaves,
   torn into pieces
12 fresh sardines
1–2 tbsp extra-virgin
   olive oil

For the tomato vinaigrette
25ml (1fl oz) extra-
   virgin olive oil
2 tbsp balsamic vinegar
1 tbsp sherry vinegar
1 tbsp capers
1½ tsp chopped tinned
   anchovy fillets
½ tsp chopped garlic
2 plum tomatoes,
   roughly chopped
Salt and black pepper

This simple Italian dish combines the freshest sardines with slightly stale bread for the 'panzanella' or bread salad. I once ate this during a trip to Tuscany and it was one of the best meals I've ever had. At this time of year, with fresh sardines and tomatoes in season, it's easy to replicate.

Combine all the ingredients for the vinaigrette in a blender or food processor and purée for 1 minute. Season with salt and pepper, to taste, and set aside.

Next, make the croutons. Preheat the oven to 200°C (400°F), Gas 6. Slice the baguette in half lengthways, rub all over with the garlic, then cut in half again lengthways. Cut these strips into 2cm (¾in) cubes and spread on a baking sheet, crust side down. Place in the oven and bake for about 3 minutes until just golden brown and crisp on the outside but still soft inside. Watch carefully as the bread can quickly burn. Remove from the oven and allow to cool.

Make up the panzanella by adding the tomato vinaigrette to a bowl and combining with the croutons, additional chopped tomatoes and the basil. Set aside for at least 20 minutes before serving, to allow the bread to soak in the dressing.

Preheat the grill to high. Lay the sardines on the grill pan, score the skins diagonally with a sharp knife, drizzle with a little olive oil and season with salt and pepper. Place under the grill and cook for 2–3 minutes on each side. Remove from the pan and serve with the bread salad on the side.

Classic chicken chasseur

Serves 4

4 plum tomatoes
50g (2oz) plain flour
1.5kg (3lb 4oz)
chicken, cut into 8
pieces, skin left on
2 tbsp olive oil
110g (4oz) butter
175g (6oz) brown cap
or button
mushrooms, halved
10 baby shallots, peeled
and halved
20g (¾oz) caster sugar
175ml (6fl oz) white
wine
450ml (16fl oz)
Chicken Stock (see
page 216)
3 tbsp tomato purée
15g (½oz) tarragon,
chopped
2 tbsp finely chopped
flat-leaf parsley
Salt and black pepper

A 1970s classic that every catering student will know only too well. If made properly, with good-quality chicken and fresh tarragon, this can be brought right up to date.

Score a cross in the bottom of each tomato, place in a bowl and cover with boiling water. Leave for 45 seconds, then drain and peel off the skin. Cut the tomatoes into quarters, remove the seeds and chop the flesh. Place the flour in another bowl and season with salt and pepper. Roll the chicken pieces in the flour, to coat, shaking off any excess.

Set a deep frying pan over a medium heat and add the oil and a third of the butter. When the butter foams, add the chicken, skin side down, and cook for 3 minutes on each side, or until golden brown. Remove the pan from the heat and set aside.

Heat another third of the butter in a separate frying pan, fry the mushrooms until golden brown, then add to the pan with the chicken. Place the remainder of the butter in the pan used for the mushrooms, add the shallots and sugar and fry for 2–3 minutes until the shallots are golden brown and caramelised. Add the wine, bring to the boil, then pour over the chicken.

Return the pan with the chicken to the heat, adding the stock, tomato purée and two-thirds of the tarragon. Bring to the boil, then reduce to a simmer and cook, uncovered, for 45 minutes to 1 hour, or until the chicken is cooked through.

Add the tomatoes, parsley and the rest of the tarragon, and season with salt and pepper. To serve, place two pieces of chicken on each plate and spoon over the sauce.

Sticky chicken wings

Serves 4

**450g (1lb) chicken
    wings**
2 tbsp coriander seeds
2 tbsp cumin seeds
**2 tbsp black mustard
    seeds**
**75g (3oz) smooth
    apricot jam**
**Zest and juice of
    2 lemons**
**50ml (2fl oz) rapeseed
    or extra-virgin olive
    oil**
Salt and black pepper

*You can get chicken wings from your butcher at a very good
price because they are the part of the bird that most people leave
behind. Serve these sticky wings with Slow-roasted Tomatoes
(see page 73).*

Bring a large saucepan of water to the boil, add the chicken
wings and simmer for 4 minutes. Remove from the water and
allow to cool.

Set a frying pan over a medium heat and add the dry spices.
When they start to pop, remove them from the pan and crush
in a blender or using a pestle and mortar.

Preheat the oven to 240°C (475°F), Gas 9. Place the crushed
spices in a large bowl, add the jam, lemon zest and juice and
the rapeseed or olive oil, season with salt and pepper and mix
well together, then add the chicken wings and stir to coat in
the spice mixture.

Place on a baking tray and roast in the oven for 15–20
minutes, or until sticky and golden brown. Remove from the
oven and serve either hot or cold.

Cold chicken breast with warm red onion and grape salad

Serves 4

1 tbsp olive oil
4 boneless, skinless
   chicken breasts
110g (4oz) white
   seedless grapes
2 red onions, peeled
   and very thinly
   sliced
Salt and black pepper

For the dressing
75ml (3fl oz) mirin
50ml (2fl oz) sake
25g (1oz) sugar
75ml (3fl oz) rice wine
   vinegar
½ green chilli, sliced

Chicken with grapes is a classic combination, and very delicious in salads. This dish is perfect for an alfresco meal on a hot summer's day. You could also make it using hot chicken straight from the barbecue.

Preheat the oven to 200°C (400°F), Gas 6.

Set a griddle pan or non-stick frying pan over a high heat, oil the chicken breasts and season them on both sides then place in the griddle pan or frying pan. Brown the chicken breasts for 3–4 minutes on each side, then transfer to the oven for 8 minutes. Remove from the oven, baste with the cooking juices from the pan and set aside to cool.

To make the dressing, place the mirin and the sake in a small saucepan set over a low heat, add the sugar and gently warm to dissolve it.

Meanwhile, cut the grapes in half and mix in a bowl with the onions. When the dressing is hot, but not boiling, add the vinegar and chilli, stir to combine, and then pour over the onions and grapes. Season well with salt and pepper and mix together.

While the salad is soaking, slice up the cooled chicken. Spoon the salad onto plates and arrange the sliced chicken on top.

Chicken with peach and watercress

Serves 4

1 tbsp olive oil
4 boneless chicken breasts, skin left on
3 sprigs of thyme, stalks removed
4 fresh peaches, quartered and stones removed
50g (2oz) watercress
50g (2oz) lamb's lettuce
Salt and black pepper

For the dressing
2 tbsp freshly squeezed orange juice
2 tbsp balsamic vinegar
2 tbsp maple syrup
4 tbsp extra-virgin olive oil

This dish has a nice mixture of contrasting textures and fresh flavours. It is best when the peaches aren't too hard, so make sure you choose ripe ones.

Preheat the oven to 200°C (400°F), Gas 6.

Add the olive oil to an ovenproof non-stick pan set over a high heat. Season the chicken with salt and pepper, sprinkle with the thyme leaves and add to the pan along with the peaches. Fry the chicken and peaches on all sides until browned, then remove the peaches and put in a separate bowl. Leave the chicken in the pan and transfer to the oven for 8–10 minutes to cook through.

Mix all the ingredients for the dressing in a bowl and season with salt and pepper. Put the watercress and lamb's lettuce in a separate bowl and mix together.

Remove the chicken from the oven and the pan and place on to plates, with the peaches and salad leaves alongside. Spoon the dressing over the chicken and the salad, grind over some pepper and serve.

Beef and fennel koftas

Serves 4

475g (1lb 1oz) minced beef
1 clove of garlic, peeled
½ tsp ground fennel
3–4 tbsp olive oil
75g (3oz) mixed salad leaves of your choice
Juice of ½ lemon
1 tbsp extra-virgin olive oil
Salt and black pepper
1 lemon, cut into wedges, to serve
4 corn on the cob, to serve

Perfect barbecue food, these beef koftas include fennel, which gives them a great flavour. I started growing fennel in the garden last year and it's extremely versatile. Pick it young to put in salads, or grill or braise it for eating warm.

Soak eight small wooden skewers for 10 minutes in cold water. Place the beef in a bowl, grate in the garlic and add the fennel. Season with salt and pepper, mix together and divide the mixture into eight pieces.

Having first dipped your hands in cold water to stop the meat sticking to them, thread each section of mince on to a wooden skewer, press into shape around the skewer and place in the fridge for 1 hour to firm up.

Set a griddle pan or frying pan over a high heat, brush each kofta with a little of the olive oil and place in the pan to cook for about 2–3 minutes on each side. Alternatively, you can cook them on a barbecue.

Place the salad leaves in a bowl and dress with the lemon juice and the extra-virgin olive oil. Season with salt and pepper and mix gently together. Remove the koftas from the pan and serve two per portion. Serve with the mixed salad, a wedge of lemon and grilled sweetcorn straight from the barbecue.

Lemon and rosemary lamb with tahini aubergines

Serves 4

12 lamb cutlets
Sprigs of mint, to serve

For the marinade
2 sprigs of rosemary,
  leaves only, finely
  chopped
Zest and juice of
  2 lemons
2 cloves of garlic,
  peeled and crushed
50ml (2fl oz) olive oil
Salt and black pepper

For the tahini aubergines
2 small aubergines or
  1 large one
2 tbsp tahini paste
Zest and juice of
  2 lemons
150ml (5fl oz) extra-
  virgin olive oil, plus
  extra for drizzling

Lamb goes brilliantly with aubergines, here soaked in a dressing made with tahini, a sesame seed paste. If you have any leftover aubergines, blend them to a purée and serve warm or cold as a sauce or a dip.

Place all the ingredients for the marinade in a bowl, season with salt and pepper and whisk together. Place the cutlets on a large plate and pour over the marinade. Rub the marinade into the lamb, place in the fridge and leave to marinate for at least 2 hours.

About an hour before you need them, slice the aubergines and season with salt and pepper. Place the tahini in a bowl, add the lemon juice and zest and the olive oil and whisk together, then pour over the aubergines.

Preheat the grill to high or light the barbecue.

Place the aubergine slices and lamb cutlets under the grill or on the barbecue and cook the aubergines for 5 minutes and the lamb for 8–10 minutes.

Remove from the grill or barbecue and arrange the aubergine slices on plates with the cutlets on the top, 3 per portion. Garnish with sprigs of mint, drizzle with olive oil and serve.

Marinated loin of lamb with warm figs, coriander and honey

Serves 4

2 x 500g (1lb 2oz) lamb loins, fat trimmed off
3 tbsp olive oil, plus extra for drizzling
4 large fresh black figs, cut into quarters
50g (2oz) rocket
1 red chilli, chopped
Salt and black pepper

For the marinade

2 cloves of garlic, peeled and chopped
1½ tbsp chopped root ginger
20g (¾oz) each of flat-leaf parsley, mint and coriander leaves, roughly chopped
½ tsp coriander seeds, crushed
60ml (2½fl oz) dark soy sauce
4 tbsp runny honey
Zest and juice of 2 limes
75ml (3fl oz) olive oil

I have a fig tree in the garden and I can't wait to harvest my first crop of fresh figs! Use ripe ones for this recipe as they go lovely and mushy when they're warmed.

To make the marinade, whizz the garlic and ginger briefly in a blender then add the remaining ingredients and blend to a paste.

Put the lamb in a large bowl and rub with three-quarters of the paste, then place in the fridge for 1 hour to marinate.

Set a non-stick frying pan over a high heat and, when hot, add 1–2 tablespoons of olive oil. Season the lamb with salt and pepper and place in the pan. Cook as you would a steak for about 4–5 minutes on each side to keep the meat pink in the middle. Once cooked, remove from the pan and set aside.

Clean the pan and return to the heat, adding the remaining olive oil. When the pan is hot, add the figs and quickly fry for no more than 1 minute.

Remove from the pan and pile on to plates. Sprinkle over the rocket and remaining marinade. Slice the lamb and divide between the plates, top with the chilli, drizzle with olive oil and serve.

Potted salt beef with gherkins

Serves 4

450g (1lb) stewing steak, cubed

¼ tsp freshly ground black pepper

¼ tsp freshly grated nutmeg

1 tbsp anchovy essence or anchovy sauce

125g (4½oz) unsalted butter, cut into cubes

½–1 tsp ground cloves

Salt

150g (5oz) gherkins, to serve

French bread, to serve

Before you ask, this is not corned beef! This recipe takes a little while to make, but it is absolutely worth the effort. Simply served with gherkins and toast or French bread, it's one of those dishes that will keep you going back to the fridge for more.

Preheat the oven to 140°C (275°F), Gas 1.

Place the beef in an ovenproof dish – preferably one with a lid. Add the pepper, nutmeg and anchovy essence, along with 110ml (4fl oz) water. Dot the butter over the top.

Cover with a lid or a double layer of foil, and place in the oven. After 1½–2 hours, remove the beef, give it a stir, then cover again and return to the oven for a further hour or until the meat is very tender.

When the beef is cooked, allow to cool, and flake into small pieces with your fingers. Add the ground cloves, to taste. Add salt if you wish, although the saltiness of the anchovy essence may be enough. Pack the mixture into ramekins or small bowls, cover with cling film, and place in the fridge to chill for 2–3 hours or preferably overnight.

Remove from the fridge and serve with gherkins and thinly sliced French bread.

Spatchcock duck with spicy tamarind glaze

Serves 4–6

1.8kg (4lb) duck, spatchcocked (see right, or ask your butcher to do this)

For the glaze
6 tbsp tamarind paste
4 tbsp runny honey
2 tsp ground coriander
1 tsp ground turmeric
Salt and black pepper

Spatchcocking is a method that can be used to prepare any type of bird. The process removes the bigger bones, making cooking and carving much easier. I've given instructions on how to spatchcock, but you can always ask the butcher to do it for you.

To spatchcock, remove the fat from just inside the cavities of the duck. Place the bird, breast side down, on a chopping board and use scissors to cut through the flesh and bone along both sides of the backbone, in a strip about 5cm (2in) wide. Cut from tail to head, completely removing the backbone.

Open out the bird, like opening a book, by gently pulling the two halves apart. Use a sharp knife to lightly score the top of the breastbone. Run your fingers along and under the sides of the breastbone and attached cartilage and pop them out. Spread the duck out flat, then turn over and make a slit about 2.5cm (1in) long in the skin between the lower end of the breastbone and the leg, on each side. Stick the end of the leg on that side through the slit and repeat on the other side.

Preheat the oven to 230°C (450°F), Gas 8 or light a barbecue. Place the duck flesh side up on a large baking tray. Place the tamarind paste in a bowl and add the honey, spices and 50ml (2fl oz) water, then season with salt and pepper. Brush half of the mixture over the skin of the duck, to completely cover.

Roast the duck in the oven for 40–50 minutes (for medium rare), or until cooked to your liking, or place on the barbecue for 20 minutes, turning every 5 minutes until well browned. Leave to rest for a few minutes before brushing with the remaining glaze. Slice the duck and serve.

Chargrilled rabbit loin with sweetcorn and chilli relish

Serves 4

4 rabbit loins, bones
   removed (ask your
   butcher to do this)
1 tbsp olive oil
25g (1oz) butter
Salt and black pepper
75g (3oz) watercress,
   to serve

For the relish
25g (1oz) caster sugar
1 plum tomato,
   roughly chopped
1 tsp chopped root
   ginger
1 clove of garlic, peeled
½ shallot, peeled and
   roughly chopped
1 tbsp Thai fish sauce
50ml (2fl oz) water
2 tbsp dark soy sauce
Zest and juice of 1 lime
2 tbsp chopped
   coriander
1 red chilli, finely
   chopped
300g tin of sweetcorn,
   drained

Because I live out in the sticks, I get given loads of rabbits for cooking. The part of the rabbit that I use most is the loin and, although it's small, it is tender and full of flavour. Be careful not to overcook it though, or it will become tough.

To make the relish, place the sugar in a medium-sized saucepan set over a medium heat. When the sugar begins to melt and darken, stir from time to time and continue to cook until it becomes a uniform liquid syrup. Meanwhile, place all the remaining ingredients, apart from the chilli and sweetcorn, in a blender and whizz to a purée.

Once the sugar has turned to a rich caramel colour (try not to let it burn), pour in the purée and mix in well. Add the chilli and bring to the boil, then reduce the heat and simmer gently for about 5 minutes.

Meanwhile, place the rabbit loins between two pieces of cling film and, using a rolling pin, flatten lightly into escalopes, then remove the cling film and season with salt and pepper. Set a non-stick frying pan over a high heat, add the olive oil and fry the loins on each side for about 2–3 minutes. Melt the butter in the pan and baste the loins with the cooking juices for a further 3–4 minutes.

Stir the sweetcorn into the chilli jam, remove the pan from the heat and serve with the rabbit and some of the watercress on the side.

Pork spare ribs with coleslaw, star anise and whisky glaze

Serves 4

1.5kg (3lb 4oz) pork spare ribs
1 tsp whole black peppercorns
1 star anise
1 onion, peeled and roughly chopped

For the glaze
200ml (7fl oz) tomato ketchup
3 star anise
150g (5oz) chipotle (hot) chilli ketchup
110ml (4fl oz) dark soy sauce
150g (5oz) runny honey
5 tbsp teriyaki sauce
6 tbsp whisky

For the coleslaw
250g (9oz) carrots, peeled
1 small onion, peeled
300g (11oz) white cabbage
250ml (9fl oz) Mayonnaise (see page 214)
Salt and black pepper

I used to wonder why those great ribs you get in the US taste so much better than the barbecue-sauce ones we have here. The answer, I discovered, is the whisky, or bourbon, that they glaze them with. So I came up with this recipe. Poaching the ribs before roasting is vital to make them all the more tender.

Place the pork ribs in a large saucepan. Add the peppercorns, star anise and onion and cover with water. Bring to the boil, then reduce the heat and simmer for 30 minutes. Remove from the heat and allow to cool in the pan, then drain the ribs.

Preheat the oven to 200°C (400°F), Gas 6. To make the glaze, place all the ingredients into another saucepan, bring to the boil and simmer for 5 minutes.

Coat the ribs in the glaze and then place on a large baking tray or roasting tin. Spoon the remaining sauce over the top and roast in the oven for 15–20 minutes. Turn occasionally to stop them burning.

Meanwhile, finely slice the carrots and onion and shred the cabbage into thin strips. Place in a bowl, add the mayonnaise, season with salt and pepper and mix together.

Remove the ribs from the oven and divide between plates. Spoon over the remaining sauce from the baking tray and serve with a dollop of coleslaw on the side.

Pan-fried pork fillet with smoky tomato sauce

Serves 4

900g (2lb) pork fillet, sliced into 8 pieces
2 tbsp olive oil
50g (2oz) butter
Salt and black pepper

For the tomato sauce
10 firm tomatoes (plum are best)
50ml (2fl oz) extra-virgin olive oil
2 shallots, peeled and finely sliced
1 red chilli, sliced
2 cloves of garlic, peeled and sliced
1 tbsp smoked paprika
20g (¾oz) coriander, chopped

The mild flavour of pork is complemented by this smoky sauce. Blasting the tomatoes may seem a bit weird, but the burnt skins create an amazing flavour. This sauce also works well with pasta.

Preheat the oven to 230°C (450°F), Gas 8. Use a rolling pin to flatten the pork slices into escalopes, each 1cm (½in) thick.

To make the sauce, spear each tomato with a fork and burn the skin with a cook's blowtorch. Alternatively, scorch under the grill. Once all the tomatoes are done, place on a baking tray and drizzle with olive oil. Place in the oven and roast for 10 minutes until soft.

Add 1 tablespoon of olive oil to a frying pan over a medium heat. When hot, add the shallots, chilli and garlic and fry for 5 minutes until the shallots are soft and brown. Add the paprika and cook for 3 more minutes, then remove from the heat and set aside.

Place the shallot mix in a blender with the cooked tomatoes and whizz briefly so that chunks of tomatoes remain. Pour into a saucepan and set over a low heat to warm through. Season with salt and pepper and add the coriander.

Season the pork escalopes well with salt and pepper. Set a frying pan over a high heat, add the olive oil and the fry the pork, lightly browning it on both sides. Add the butter, basting the pork with the cooking juices, then reduce the heat and allow to cook through for 3–4 minutes.

Place each escalope on a plate, spooning the sauce on the side, and serve with either jacket or sautéed potatoes.

Poached cherries
with almond glaze

Serves 4

**200ml (7fl oz) good-
quality red wine**
75g (3oz) caster sugar
**2 vanilla pods, each cut
in two**
**450g (1lb) English
cherries, stones
removed**
**25g (1oz) flaked
almonds, toasted
(see page 181)**

For the almond glaze
1 egg, white and yolk
3 egg yolks
200g (7oz) caster sugar
**50g (2oz) ground
almonds**

*Fresh cherries are best for this but you could also use tinned ones that
have been drained well. Either way, serve the pudding straight from
the grill to the table, with lashings of double cream or ice cream.*

Place the wine, sugar and vanilla pods and scraped-out seeds
in a large, heavy-based frying pan and bring to the boil. When
the sugar has dissolved, pop the cherries into the cooking
liquid, bring back up to the boil, then remove from the heat.

Remove the cherries from the cooking liquid, set the pan back
over the heat and simmer until the wine mixture reduces to a
syrup. Remove from the heat and allow to cool, then place
the cherries back in the syrup and set aside.

Half fill a medium-sized saucepan with boiling water and
set over a low heat so that it simmers. Place a similar-sized
bowl on top, making sure the bottom of the bowl does not
touch the water. Add the whole egg, the egg yolks and sugar
and whisk together until the mixture has doubled in size.
Remove the bowl from the pan and continue to whisk for
about 5 minutes or until the eggs become whitish in colour,
then fold in the ground almonds.

Preheat the grill to high. Keeping the poached cherries in the
pan, or transferring them to a heatproof serving dish, carefully
spoon over the almond glaze to cover the fruit. Place under
the grill for 2–3 minutes to allow to brown. Remove from
the grill, sprinkle with the toasted almonds and serve.

Black cherry brownies

Serves 8

**350g (12oz) dark
chocolate (55–60%
cocoa solids),
broken into pieces**
**250g (9oz) unsalted
butter**
3 eggs
**250g (9oz) dark soft
brown sugar**
**110g (4oz) plain flour,
sifted**
1 tsp baking powder
Pinch of salt
**175g (6oz) fresh
cherries, stones
removed**

*Yeah, yeah, I know there are loads of brownie recipes out there.
So what makes this one special? Nothing in particular, but I've
spent twenty years as a pastry chef and this is my favourite. If you
can't find fresh cherries, use strawberries or raspberries instead.*

Preheat the oven to 170°C (325°F), Gas 3 and butter a 23cm
(9in) square cake tin.

Place the chocolate and butter in a saucepan set over a low
heat and gently melt, stirring occasionally. Remove from the
heat and allow to cool slightly.

Whisk the eggs until thick, then gradually add the sugar and
beat until glossy. Beat in the melted chocolate mixture, then
gently fold in the flour, baking powder and salt.

Pour just over half the mixture into the prepared cake tin.
Scatter over the stoned cherries, then cover with the
remaining mixture.

Bake in the oven for about 40 minutes or until the surface is
set. The brownies will be cooked when a skewer inserted into
the middle comes out with just a little mixture adhering.

Remove from the oven, place the tin on a wire rack, and allow
to rest for about 20 minutes. Cut the brownies into squares
and carefully remove them from the tin when cold.

Eggy croissants with fresh raspberries and zabaglione

Serves 4

2 eggs
200ml (7fl oz) milk
75g (3oz) caster sugar
1 vanilla pod
4 croissants
50g (2oz) butter
**400g (14oz) fresh
   raspberries**

For the zabaglione
2 egg yolks
2 tbsp caster sugar
**50ml (2fl oz) sweet
   sherry or Marsala**

I love eggy bread, and this version made with croissants is particularly indulgent. Zabaglione is a lightly whisked tangy custard, traditionally flavoured with Marsala wine and served with figs. I always make this with the finest Scottish raspberries, but ones from the garden are just fine!

Lightly whisk the eggs in a large bowl and then mix in the milk and the sugar. Split the vanilla pod in half and scrape the seeds into the mixture, then add both halves of the vanilla pod. Cut the croissants in half horizontally and soak in the egg mixture for about a minute, then set aside on a large plate.

To make the zabaglione, half fill a saucepan with boiling water and set over a low heat so that it simmers. Place a similar-sized bowl on the top, making sure the bottom of the bowl does not touch the water. Add all the ingredients for the zabaglione and whisk well for 2–3 minutes until light and frothy.

Set a large frying pan over a high heat and, when hot, add half the butter. As soon as the butter is frothy and starting to go brown, place four croissant halves in the pan and cook for about 30 seconds on each side until they are golden brown. Repeat with the remaining croissant halves.

Place the croissants on plates, drizzle with the zabaglione, scatter the raspberries over the top and serve immediately.

Oven-roasted apricots with honey madeleines

Serves 4

500g (1lb 2oz) fresh apricots
50g (2oz) butter
1 vanilla pod
50g (2oz) runny honey
1 sprig of thyme, leaves only

For the madeleines
250g (9oz) plain flour, sifted
375g (13oz) caster sugar
1 tsp vanilla extract
3 eggs
2 tbsp runny honey
225g (8oz) unsalted butter, melted

This is best made with fresh apricots, but if you can't get hold of them, you can substitute with other stoned fruit, or even tinned apricots. Madeleines are little cakes which come from the north-east of France and are traditionally baked in shell-like moulds. You can buy these moulds from any good cookshop or try looking in an antique shop for one with character.

Preheat the oven to 170°C (325°F), Gas 3.

To make the madeleines, place the flour and 250g (9oz) sugar in a large bowl and add the vanilla extract, eggs, honey and melted butter. Mix well together and spoon into a madeleine tin. Bake for 15–20 minutes, depending on the size of the cakes, until golden brown.

Meanwhile, cut each apricot in half and remove the stone. Set an ovenproof pan over a low–medium heat, add half the butter and, when it has melted, add the apricots and briefly fry until lightly browned.

Slice the vanilla pod in half lengthways and add both pieces to the pan along with the honey, the thyme leaves and the rest of the butter. Stir to coat the apricots and then transfer the pan to the oven to cook for 10 minutes.

Remove the madeleines from the oven. Remove from the tin and, while still warm, roll in the remaining caster sugar. Take the cooked apricots out of the oven and spoon into bowls with the sauce from the pan drizzled over the top. Serve with the madeleines alongside.

Lemon verbena cake with strawberries and cream

Serves 6–8

200g (7oz) self-raising flour, sifted
12 lemon verbena leaves
1 tsp baking powder
4 medium eggs
200g (7oz) butter, softened, plus extra for greasing
200g (7oz) caster sugar
½ tsp vanilla extract

For the filling
150g (5oz) mascarpone
3 tbsp icing sugar
150ml (5fl oz) double cream
300g (11oz) fresh strawberries, hulled and sliced

To decorate
12 small strawberries, left whole
2 sprigs lemon verbena
Icing sugar, for dusting

Lemon verbena is a herb that can be used in many sweet and savoury dishes and is delicious in tea, ice cream or crème brûlée. It is particularly good in a cake – its lemony flavour will keep people guessing.

Preheat the oven to 170°C (325°F), Gas 3. Butter two 20cm x 4cm (8in x 1½in) sandwich tins and line the bases with greaseproof paper.

To make the cake, place the flour and lemon verbena in a food processor and blitz for 1 minute. Add all the other cake ingredients and blend again for 1 minute. Alternatively, finely chop the lemon verbena and add to a large bowl with the remaining ingredients, then mix together using a hand-held electric beater. The consistency is right if the mixture just drops off a tablespoon tapped on the side of the bowl. Add a little milk if the mixture is too stiff or extra flour if it is sloppy.

Divide the mixture between the two tins, smooth the tops of the cakes so that they are level and place on the centre shelf of the oven. Cook for 30–35 minutes, but don't open the oven door for 30 minutes or the cakes may collapse.

To test whether the cakes are cooked, lightly press the centre of each with your finger: if it leaves no impression and the sponge springs back slightly, the cakes are ready.

Remove the cakes from the oven, then wait about 5 minutes before turning them out on to a wire rack. Allow to cool slightly, then remove the paper from the base of each cake and leave to cool fully.

To make the filling, place the mascarpone in a bowl with the icing sugar and mix well. Pour in the cream and stir together until the mixture forms soft peaks.

Place one sponge on a cake board or serving plate and spread the cream mixture over the top. Add the sliced strawberries and top with the remaining sponge. Dust with icing sugar and decorate with the small strawberries and lemon verbena leaves.

Teacakes with warm strawberries and clotted cream

Makes 8–10 teacakes

400g (14oz) plain flour, sifted, plus extra for dusting

½ tsp salt

40g (1½oz) caster sugar

1 tsp cinnamon

½ tsp mixed spice

50g (2oz) butter, softened, plus extra for greasing

25g (1oz) dried yeast

75g (3oz) sultanas

60g (2½oz) mixed peel

1 egg yolk, lightly beaten, for brushing

To serve

25g (1oz) butter

25g (1oz) caster sugar

200g (7oz) fresh strawberries, hulled and halved

200g (7oz) clotted cream

Not as sweet as a hot-cross bun, but still with a nice spicy taste. Teacakes come in many varieties – in Yorkshire we sometimes leave out the dried fruit, and in Kent they are flavoured with hops and called 'huffkins'. This recipe is a teacake take on the classic British cream tea.

Place the flour, salt, sugar, spices, butter and yeast in a large bowl. Add 225ml (8fl oz) warm water (although you may need more, depending on the absorbency of the flour) and mix together to form a dough.

Knead for 4–5 minutes in the bowl then transfer on to a floured work surface. Knead the dough for a further 6–8 minutes, then place back in the bowl, cover with a clean tea towel and leave for 1 hour to rise.

Add the sultanas and mixed peel to the dough, kneading to incorporate, and divide the dough into pieces each weighing about 75g (3oz). Shape into balls and use a rolling pin or the palm of your hand to flatten them to 1cm (½in) thick. Place the uncooked teacakes on a buttered baking tray and leave in a warm place to rise for a further hour.

Preheat the oven to 190°C (375°F), Gas 5. Brush the teacakes with beaten egg and bake for 15 minutes. While they are cooking, heat the butter and sugar (for serving) in a small frying pan set over a low heat and sauté the strawberries for 1 minute, then remove from the heat.

Remove the teacakes from the oven and serve with clotted cream and the warm strawberries.

Spiced redcurrant jelly

Makes 2.5 litres
(4⅓ pints)

**1.5kg (3lb 4oz)
  redcurrants
3 cloves
1 tsp cinnamon
250ml (9fl oz) malt
  vinegar
1.5kg (3lb 4oz) jam
  sugar**

*I love making chutneys and jams but a clear jelly requires time
and patience. Allow the fruit to strain slowly and don't rush the
process by trying to push it through the bag, or it will cause the
mixture to go cloudy. If stored in properly sealed jars, the jelly
will keep for at least a year. It's great served with game or lamb,
or spread on scones.*

Put the redcurrants into a large pan as they are – no need to
remove the berries from the stalks, or any leaves that are still
attached. Add 1 litre (1¾ pints) water and the spices.

Bring to the boil, reduce the heat and simmer for 6–7 minutes
until the redcurrants are soft. Remove from the heat and
strain through a jelly bag into another pan. This will take a
few hours. Alternatively, and if you don't mind cloudy-
looking jelly, strain through a sieve.

Add the vinegar and sugar to the strained liquid in the pan
and boil for 8–10 minutes until the setting point is reached.
Spoon a little of the liquid on to a cold plate, allow to cool
briefly in the fridge, then see if your finger, drawn through the
centre, leaves a clear line that doesn't fill back in. If not, cook
the jelly for a further 15 minutes, then repeat the setting test.

When the setting point has been reached, pour the jelly into
sterilised jam jars (see page 166) and seal while still very hot.

Sweet and sour pickled plums

*Makes 2 x 1 litre
(1¾ pint) jars*

**1kg (2lb 2oz) plums,
halved and stones
removed**
10 allspice berries
4 cloves
1 star anise
1 cinnamon stick
**425ml (15fl oz) white
wine vinegar**
225g (8oz) caster sugar
1 red chilli
**1¾ tbsp chopped root
ginger**

*These plums, presented in a handsome jar, make a great gift
as well as being a good way to keep and store a glut of summer
plums. If you have plum trees, like me, you have to be quick
and pick them before the wasps get there first.*

Place the plums in a large pan, adding just enough water
to cover them, bring to the boil, then turn the heat down
to low and gently simmer for 5–6 minutes.

Remove from the heat, lift the plums from the water and
place them into sterilised pickling jars (for sterilising jars,
see page 166). Drain off half the water and add the rest of
the ingredients to the pan.

Return to the heat, bring back up to the boil and allow to
cook for 10 minutes. Remove from the heat and pour over
the plums. Put the lids on the jars and store in a cool, dry
place with no direct sunlight. Stored properly, the plums
will last for 5–6 months.

Autumn

**Pumpkins • Mushrooms • Beetroot • Pears
Apples • Hazelnuts • Damsons • Lemon sole
Haddock • Wild grouse • Venison • Rabbit**

As the leaves begin to drop, the food just keeps on growing. Pumpkins are round and ripe, apples and pears are ready to be picked and wild mushrooms are waiting to be foraged. You're lucky if you have a plum or sloe tree in your garden, as it will be heaving with fruit – great for making jelly or jam. The nut trees are also full of offerings. Autumn is an interesting time for seafood, with clams, haddock and lemon sole. And it's the start of the game season, with venison and the famous wild grouse.

Pumpkin soup with chestnut cream

Serves 4
Vegetarian

700g (1lb 8oz)
pumpkin or
butternut squash
1 medium onion,
peeled and chopped
1 clove of garlic, peeled
and chopped
2 tbsp extra-virgin
olive oil
75g (3oz) pre-cooked
chestnuts
200ml (7fl oz) double
cream
750ml (26fl oz)
Vegetable or Chicken
Stock (see pages 218
and 216)
110ml (4fl oz) white
wine
50g (2oz) butter, cut in
pieces
Salt and black pepper

A good tip with all squash-based soups is to add plenty of salt – the veg needs it. You can buy ready-cooked chestnuts, but if you want to roast your own, cut a small cross in the top of each one (to prevent them from exploding), place on a baking tray and bake in the oven at 200°C (400°F), Gas 6 for 30 minutes. Serve the soup with chunks of crusty bread.

Preheat the oven to 200°C (400°F), Gas 6. Peel the pumpkin with a potato peeler and cut into 5cm (2in) chunks. Place on a baking tray or in a roasting tin, sprinkle over the onion and garlic and drizzle with the olive oil to coat all the vegetables. Roast in the oven for 30 minutes, or until softened.

While the pumpkin is cooking, chop the chestnuts. In a large bowl, whisk a third of the cream into soft peaks and then fold in half the chestnuts. Leave in the fridge until needed.

Warm the stock to simmering point in a large saucepan set over a medium heat. When the pumpkin is ready, remove from the oven, sprinkle with the white wine and tip into the hot stock in the pan.

Add the butter and the remaining cream to the soup, then pour into a blender and whizz to a purée, or use a hand-held blender to blitz. Return to the pan and reheat gently, then season with salt and pepper, place in bowls and spoon dollops of the chilled chestnut cream mixture on top. Sprinkle with the remaining chestnuts and serve.

Hazelnut-coated goat's cheese with lemon and beetroot salad

Serves 4
Vegetarian

**8 medium, fresh
  beetroot**
**75g (3oz) whole
  hazelnuts, skinned
  (for skinning, see
  page 30)**
1 egg white
**2 logs of Peroche goat's
  cheese**
**4 slices of crusty white
  bread**
**Zest and juice of
  2 lemons**
**3 tbsp extra-virgin
  olive oil**
3 tbsp hazelnut oil
**110g (4oz) mixed frisée
  lettuce and red
  mustard leaves**
Salt and black pepper

I was never a massive fan of goat's cheese (or goats themselves, come to that!) until I discovered Peroche goat's cheese. It's made by Neal's Yard (see Supplier list on page 219), and is very high in moisture, so isn't at all chalky in taste. It should be eaten very fresh. If you can't get hold of it, use any similar log of good-quality soft goat's cheese.

To cook the beetroot for the salad, place in a large saucepan of cold water, add a good pinch of salt, bring to the boil and cook for 30–40 minutes. Allow to cool, then peel and set aside.

Preheat the grill to high, then place the hazelnuts in a blender and blitz to a crumb. Empty the chopped nuts on to a plate.

Place the egg white in a bowl and whisk with a fork just to break it up. Roll the goat's cheese in the egg and then in the hazelnuts, coating well with chopped nuts. Then, using a sharp knife dipped in hot water, cut each goat's cheese in half (the Peroche log slices into 2 x 1cm (½in) pieces).

Cut the bread into croutons the same diameter as the cheese, toast briefly under the grill, then remove and place the cheese cut-side up on top. Place on a baking tray and return to the hot grill to cook for 3–4 minutes.

Meanwhile, place the lemon zest and juice in a bowl, mix in the olive and hazelnut oils, and season with salt and pepper, to taste. To serve, slice the beetroot and arrange in the middle of each plate. Add the salad leaves, spoon over the dressing and place the hot goat's cheese croutons on top.

Cromer crab toastie

Serves 2

1 dressed Cromer crab or 150g (5oz) mixed crab meat, white and dark
3 tbsp crème fraîche
1 tsp dark soy sauce
Splash of Tabasco sauce (optional)
3 tbsp chopped chives
50g (2oz) butter
4 thin slices of white bread
Salt and black pepper
1 lemon, cut into wedges, to serve

To garnish
Leaves from 1 Little Gem lettuce
1 plum tomato, thinly sliced
2 tbsp Vinaigrette (see page 212)

Here's a nice simple snack to have at lunchtime and, to make it even easier, it can be made using frozen crab meat, if you prefer. For an extra kick, add a pinch of curry powder to the crab mixture.

Place the crab meat in a bowl, then check to make sure all the tiny pieces of shell have been removed. Mix in the crème fraîche, soy sauce, Tabasco (if using) and chives. Season with salt and pepper, to taste.

Preheat the grill to high and toast the bread under the grill. Butter the toast, add the crab mixture to one slice and sandwich together with another slice, then repeat to make the second sandwich. Alternatively, butter the untoasted bread on both sides and place two pieces into a toasted-sandwich maker. Add the crab mixture and top with the other two pieces of buttered bread. Place the lid down and toast according to the manufacturer's instructions, then remove from the machine.

Cut each sandwich into four and serve with the lettuce leaves and tomato slices, dressed with the vinaigrette, plus a lemon wedge for squeezing over the crab mixture.

Scrambled duck eggs with crispy bacon and watercress

Serves 4

8 duck eggs
110ml (4fl oz) double cream
50g (2oz) butter, softened
8 rashers of smoked, dry-cured streaky bacon
60g (2½oz) watercress
Salt and black pepper

A great way to cook scrambled eggs is to soft-boil them in their shells before scrambling in a pan. I first saw it done by Jason Atherton, the chef at Maze, and thanks to him I've made them this way ever since.

Bring a large saucepan of salted water to the boil. Place the duck eggs in the water, lowering in each one carefully with a spoon to stop them cracking, reduce the heat and simmer gently for 7–8 minutes to soft-boil the eggs.

Remove the pan from the heat, drain off the water and place the eggs under running water until cold, to stop them cooking further. Peel off the shells, then slice each egg in half and scoop out the runny yolks into a large bowl.

Preheat the grill to high. Finely dice the egg whites and add to a frying pan set over a low heat. Add the cream and butter and warm through. Meanwhile, place the bacon under the grill and cook on both sides until nice and crispy.

Remove the pan from the heat and stir in the runny yolks, season with salt and pepper and place on plates with the slices of bacon and a pile of watercress on the side.

Marinated mackerel with horseradish and crusty bread

Serves 4

4 fresh mackerel fillets, skin left on
275g (10oz) caster sugar
275ml (10fl oz) white wine vinegar
2 bay leaves
1 tbsp allspice
1 tbsp yellow mustard seeds
½ tbsp caraway seeds
1 tbsp pink peppercorns
50g (2oz) dill, chopped
2 shallots, peeled and sliced into rings
75g (3oz) frisée lettuce
10 chervil leaves
Crusty bread, to serve

For the dressing
2 tsp Creamed Horseradish (shop-bought or see page 213)
50ml (2fl oz) single cream
Juice of ½ lemon
Salt and black pepper

Fresh horseradish and mackerel make a perfect pair, but don't, whatever you do, plant horseradish in your garden or you'll never get rid of the stuff. Instead, get it from a local vegetable supplier or your supermarket.

Place the mackerel fillets in a dish so they fit snugly, skin side down, filling the bottom of the dish. Pour 150ml (5fl oz) water into a small saucepan set over a low heat, add the sugar and vinegar, and warm through to dissolve the sugar. Add the bay leaves, spices and peppercorns, remove from the heat and allow to cool.

Sprinkle the dill and shallots over the fish, pour over the marinade and cover with cling film. Place in the fridge and allow to chill for about 3 hours.

Place the frisée leaves in a bowl. Mix together in a cup or small bowl the creamed horseradish, cream and lemon juice, season with salt and pepper and pour over the salad. Add the chervil leaves and toss together to coat evenly with the dressing.

To serve, arrange the salad on plates with slices of the bread. Remove the fish from the fridge and add to the plates, skin side up. Place some of the shallot rings on the top and drizzle over a little of the marinade.

Pan-fried lemon sole with clams, coriander and tomato

Serves 4

450g (1lb) clams
8 x 75–110g (3–4oz)
  lemon sole fillets
125ml (4½fl oz) olive
  oil
½ tsp coriander seeds,
  crushed
2 shallots, peeled and
  finely sliced into
  rings
1 garlic clove, peeled
  and lightly crushed
  but left whole
Zest and juice of
  1 lemon
4 ripe tomatoes,
  skinned, deseeded
  and finely chopped
  (see method page 83)
2 tbsp roughly chopped
  flat-leaf parsley
½ bunch coriander
Salt and black pepper

Always delicious, lemon sole is even better served with clams. (But forget those awful pickled clams you get on the seafront in styrofoam containers with a mini pitchfork stuck in the top!) If you can't get clams, you can use mussels instead.

Place the clams in a colander and wash them thoroughly under running water, discarding any with broken shells or which don't close when tapped against the side of the colander.

Set a frying pan with a lid over a high heat. Add the clams and 110ml (4fl oz) water and cover with the lid. Steam the clams for 2 minutes until they have all opened up. Discard any that have not opened and pour the contents of the pan into a colander set over a bowl or saucepan. Remove the clam flesh from the shells, discarding the shells but keeping the cooking liquid.

Season the sole fillets with salt and pepper. Set a separate frying pan over a medium–high heat, add 1 tablespoon of the olive oil and the sole fillets. Fry for 1–2 minutes on each side, or until just cooked through. Remove the sole from the pan and place on a plate to prevent them from cooking any further.

Pour the reserved cooking liquid into the pan and stir over a medium heat to deglaze, loosening and incorporating any sediment from the bottom of the pan with a wooden spoon. Increase the heat and simmer the liquid to reduce by half, then remove from the heat and set aside.

To make the sauce, place the remaining olive oil in a saucepan set over a low heat. Add the coriander seeds, shallots, garlic and clams and cook for 1 minute. Season, to taste, with salt and pepper, then add the lemon zest and juice and remove from the heat.

Place the tomatoes in a bowl along with the parsley and coriander leaves and the reduced liquid from the clams. Pour over the sauce and stir gently. To serve, first remove the whole garlic clove from the bowl, then place the sole fillets on plates with the finished sauce spooned over the top.

Herb-crusted cod with spicy cauliflower cheese

Serves 4

4 x 175g (6oz) cod fillet steaks
75g (3oz) butter, cut into pieces
1 small cauliflower, cut into florets
110ml (4fl oz) double cream
150g (5oz) Comté or Gruyère cheese, grated
¼ tsp cayenne pepper
Salt and black pepper

For the crust
75g (3oz) dried breadcrumbs, such as Japanese panko
30g (1¼oz) flat-leaf parsley, chopped
50g (2oz) butter, melted

I came up with this recipe when I was cooking for a dinner party and accidentally overcooked the cauli. The method below results in a slightly chunky cauliflower cheese, but if you're pushed for time you can pop the cauliflower in a blender with cream, butter, cheese and seasoning and you end up with a smooth, cheesy cauliflower purée.

Preheat the oven to 200°C (400°F), Gas 6.

To make the crust, place the breadcrumbs and parsley in a bowl and stir in the melted butter to make a dough.

Place the fish on a baking tray or roasting tin, season with salt and pepper and top with the crust, spreading the dough over each steak to a thickness of about 3–4mm (⅛in). Dot over a third of the butter and bake in the oven for 15 minutes.

Meanwhile, bring a large saucepan of water to the boil, season with salt and add the cauliflower florets. Boil for 5–6 minutes until quite soft but not too overcooked. Remove from the heat, drain and place the florets back in the pan.

Using a potato masher, mash the cauliflower in the pan with the remaining butter, then add the cream, cheese and cayenne and season with salt and pepper, to taste. Keep warm.

Remove the fish from the oven and serve with the cauliflower purée, reheated if necessary, and melted butter from the baking tray spooned over the top.

Smoked haddock, leek and mascarpone tart

Serves 6

225g (8oz) ready-made shortcrust pastry, at room temperature

Flour, for dusting

50g (2oz) butter, plus extra for greasing

2 trimmed leeks, finely sliced

300g (11oz) natural smoked haddock

3–4 tbsp olive oil

250ml (9fl oz) double cream

50g (2oz) mascarpone

1 whole egg

2 egg yolks

4 tbsp chopped flat-leaf parsley

Salt and black pepper

Don't buy that yellow-dyed haddock from the fish counter – the paler natural type has a subtler flavour and is more attractive. My favourite are Arbroath Smokies (see Supplier list on page 219).

Preheat the oven to 200°C (400°F), Gas 6. Grease a 20cm x 2.5cm (8in x 1in) loose-bottomed tart tin and roll out the pastry on a lightly floured surface. Lay the pastry over the tin and press it gently into the base and sides. Trim off any excess, cover the lined tin with foil or cling film and chill in the fridge for 30 minutes.

Remove the tart case from the fridge and line with greaseproof paper. Fill with baking beans or uncooked rice and bake 'blind' for 15 minutes. Remove the beans and the greaseproof paper and return the tart case to the oven to bake for a further 5–6 minutes, or until just cooked and turning golden brown.

Reduce the oven temperature to 180°C (350°F), Gas 4. Meanwhile, melt the butter in a large, deep frying pan set over a low heat. Add the leeks and fry until just softened. Remove from the heat and allow to cool.

Place the haddock on a baking tray, sprinkle with the olive oil and place in the oven for 6–7 minutes, then remove and flake into big chunks, discarding any bones.

Place the cream, mascarpone, whole egg and egg yolks in a bowl and whisk to combine. Add the egg and cream mixture to the cooled leeks and mix together. Add the haddock flakes and the parsley and season well with salt and pepper. Pour the mixture into the baked tart case and bake in the oven for 20 minutes, or until the filling is set and the top is golden brown.

Salmon and pumpkin risotto

Serves 4

**300g (11oz) pumpkin
  or butternut squash**
1–2 tbsp olive oil
50g (2oz) butter
200g (7oz) Arborio rice
**500ml (18fl oz) Fish
  Stock (see page 217)**
**4 x 200g (7oz) salmon
  fillets**
2 tsp mascarpone
**2 tbsp freshly grated
  Parmesan cheese**
3 tsp double cream
**1–2 tbsp chilli oil
  (optional)**
Salt and black pepper

*Another risotto recipe? (See Smoked Haddock, Globe Artichoke
and Lemon Risotto, page 76.) But why not? Risottos are so easy
to make and can be adapted for any time of year. This is one of
my favourite recipes in the whole book, so much so that it hasn't
been off my bistro menu for a year.*

Preheat the oven to 180°C (350°F), Gas 4. Peel the pumpkin
with a potato peeler and cut into 5cm (2in) chunks. Place
on a baking tray or in a roasting tin, drizzle with the olive
oil and roast in the oven for 30 minutes, or until softened
and lightly browned. Place in a blender (or use a hand-held
blender) and purée.

Meanwhile, melt half the butter in a large saucepan set over
a medium heat, add the rice and stir with the butter for
1 minute. Adding the stock a little at a time, cook the rice
for 12 minutes. Once cooked, and all the liquid has been
absorbed, remove from the heat and set aside to cool.

Set a non-stick frying pan over a medium heat, add the
salmon fillets and cook on both sides to seal. Melt the
remaining butter in the pan and cook the salmon for 5–6
minutes, basting with the butter, then remove the pan from
the heat and set aside.

Stir the pumpkin purée into the cooked rice, add mascarpone
and Parmesan and season with salt and pepper. Set the pan
over a medium heat and cook for 3–4 minutes, then stir in
the cream and allow to heat through for another 1–2 minutes.

Serve the salmon fillets on top of the pumpkin risotto and
drizzle with the chilli oil.

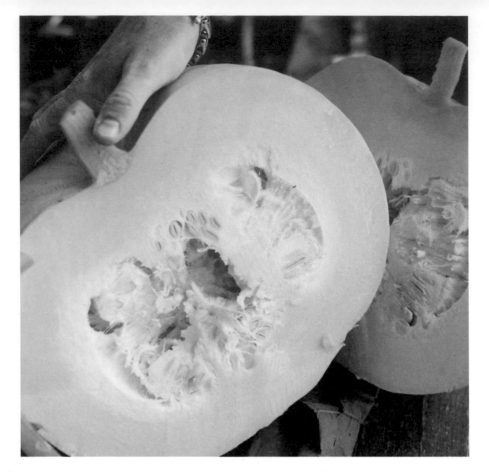

Pot-roasted chicken with pumpkin, sage and star anise

Serves 4

4–5 tbsp olive oil
110g (4oz) butter
**4 boneless, skinless
    chicken breasts**
**800g (1¾lb) pumpkin,
    peeled and cut into
    1cm (½in) cubes**
4 sprigs of sage
**1 lemon, cut into
    quarters**
3 tsp ground star anise
Salt and black pepper

Pumpkin goes well with most flavours, including sage, almonds and even Amaretti biscuits, but if you're serving it with meat or fish, I would recommend the exotic flavour of star anise to complement it best.

Set a large frying pan with a lid over a high heat and add 2–3 tablespoons of olive oil and half the butter. Season the chicken with salt and pepper and, when the butter has melted, add the chicken to the pan and brown on both sides. Remove from the pan and set aside.

Add the remaining olive oil and butter to the same pan used for the chicken. Tip in the pumpkin cubes and sauté for 2–3 minutes, then add the sage, lemon wedges and enough water to half cover the pumpkin. Place the chicken breasts on the top, cover with the lid and cook gently for 20 minutes.

Once the chicken is cooked, but the pumpkin cubes are still retaining their shape, remove the chicken and set aside to rest. Turn up the heat under the pan, add the star anise and cook for 4–5 minutes. Season with salt and pepper and add more butter, to taste, if needed. Slice the chicken breasts, spoon the pumpkin sauce on to plates, with a lemon quarter per plate, and arrange the chicken on top.

Pan-fried chicken with Waldorf salad

Serves 2

2 boneless, skinless chicken breasts
1 tbsp olive oil
20g (¾oz) butter
Salt and black pepper

For the Waldorf salad
2 tbsp light soft brown sugar
25g (1oz) butter
75g (3oz) shelled walnut halves
1 dessert apple (Granny Smith or another sweet, tart variety)
1 stick of celery, chopped into 1cm (½in) cubes
Juice of ½ lemon
4 tbsp Mayonnaise (good-quality shop-bought or see page 214)
20g (¾oz) sultanas
Leaves of 1 Little Gem lettuce

Invented at the Waldorf Hotel in New York, this classic salad is over a hundred years old and still going strong. It's a must for the apple season. This version uses delicious sugar-coated walnuts.

Put the chicken breasts on a chopping board and, using a sharp knife, cut them horizontally, not all the way through, but just enough to open each out into an escalope. Place the flattened-out chicken breasts in between two layers of cling film and use a rolling pin to flatten them a little further. Remove the cling film and season the chicken with salt and pepper.

Set a frying pan over a medium–high heat, add the olive oil and the butter and, when the butter has melted, fry the chicken for 3–4 minutes on each side.

While the chicken is cooking, start making the Waldorf salad. Place another frying pan over a medium heat and add the sugar and butter. When the butter turns brown and starts to caramelise, add the walnuts and sauté for 3–4 minutes to brown and coat in the butter and sugar. Remove from the pan and set aside to cool.

Peel the apple, core it and chop into 1cm (½in) cubes, then place the apple and celery pieces in a bowl. Add the lemon juice, mayonnaise and sultanas. Add the cooled walnuts, mix well and season with salt and pepper. Slice the lettuce leaves and mix in with the salad.

Place the chicken on plates and serve with the Waldorf salad.

Fillet of beef with beetroot and parsley

Serves 4

**350g (12oz) fresh
beetroot**
**2 tsp Pommery
mustard or other
wholegrain mustard**
**4 x 200g (7oz) thick
fillet steaks**
**5g (¼oz) thyme leaves,
chopped**
**5g (¼oz) chervil leaves,
chopped**
**1 tbsp olive oil
(optional)**
**2 cloves of garlic,
peeled and finely
chopped**
**50ml (2fl oz) extra-
virgin olive oil**
Juice of 1 lemon
**30g (1¼oz) flat-leaf
parsley**
Salt and black pepper

Millions of tons of beets are grown in the UK each year – not just for the supermarkets, but also for animal food or to turn into sugar. Chard is actually a variety of beet, but it's the red beet that we use most in the kitchen. If you're cooking it from raw, wait until after it's cooked to peel it.

Place the beetroot in a large saucepan of cold water, add a good pinch of salt, bring to the boil and cook for 30–40 minutes. Allow to cool and then peel and set aside.

Spread some of the mustard over one side of each of the fillet steaks. Mix the thyme and chervil with the chopped garlic, then sprinkle the mixture over the steaks so that it sticks to the mustard. Season with salt and pepper.

Set a large, non-stick frying pan over a high heat (depending on the pan, you may need to add a little olive oil) and fry the steaks for a few minutes per side, according to your liking – 2 minutes per side for rare, 3 minutes for medium and 5 minutes for well done. Remove from the heat and set aside to rest.

Chop the cooked beetroot and then mix with the extra-virgin olive oil, lemon juice and parsley. Season with salt and pepper. Place a spoonful of beetroot salad on to each plate and the fillet steak alongside. Serve immediately.

Rib-eye steak with stick fries and Chateaubriand sauce

Serves 4

4 large baking potatoes
1.2 litres (2 pints) vegetable oil, if deep-frying, or 2 tbsp olive oil, if baking
4 x 200g (7oz) rib-eye steaks
3 tbsp olive oil
50g (2oz) butter
Salt and black pepper

For the sauce
1½ litres (2½ pints) Chicken Stock (see page 216)
110g (4oz) butter
1 clove of garlic, peeled and chopped
4 shallots, peeled and thinly sliced
300g (11oz) button mushrooms, sliced
200ml (7fl oz) white wine
1 small bunch of tarragon, leaves only, chopped

There's no better way to serve steak than with this old-fashioned sauce. It needs a lot of fresh stock, but as you reduce it and add the butter, it will get lovely and thick and full of flavour.

To make the sauce, pour the stock into a large saucepan, bring to the boil and simmer to reduce it by four-fifths or until there is about 250ml (9fl oz) left. Remove from the heat and set aside.

To make the chips, peel the potatoes and cut into matchsticks. If using a deep-fat fryer, heat the vegetable oil to 190°C (375°F). Alternatively, fill a deep, heavy-based frying pan to a depth of 2cm (¾in) with oil and use a sugar thermometer to check that it has reached the correct temperature. For cooking the chips in the oven, preheat the oven to 180°C (350°C), Gas 4.

Set a large frying pan over a high heat, and season the steaks well with salt and pepper. Add the olive oil and butter to the pan and, when the butter starts to foam, add the steaks. For rare, cook on each side for 2 minutes; for medium, cook for 3 minutes; or for well done, cook for 5 minutes. Remove from the heat and set aside to rest.

To make the sauce, place another frying pan on the hob, set over a medium–high heat, add 25g (1oz) butter and sauté the garlic and shallots. Add the mushrooms, then quickly add the wine and half the tarragon, followed by the reduced stock.

Reduce the sauce until thickened, then remove from the heat and whisk in the remaining butter. Add the remaining tarragon, season with salt and pepper and set aside.

To deep-fry the chips, drop into the hot vegetable oil and fry for 4–5 minutes until golden brown, then remove from the oil, dry on kitchen paper and season with sea salt. To cook the chips in the oven, lay the cut potatoes on a baking sheet. Drizzle with olive oil, season with sea salt and bake for 8–10 minutes, turning occasionally, until cooked.

Serve the chips immediately with the steak and the sauce spooned on the side.

Pan-fried calf's liver with cider-battered onion rings

Serves 4

50g (2oz) butter
700g (1½lb) calf's liver, thinly sliced
50g (2oz) flour, for dusting
12 large sage leaves
150ml (5fl oz) Madeira
900ml (1½ pints) beef or Chicken Stock (see page 216)
Sea salt and black pepper

For the battered onion rings
1.2 litres (2 pints) vegetable oil, for deep-frying
150g (5oz) plain flour
1 tsp sea salt
300ml (11fl oz) Scrumpy Jack cider
2 medium onions, peeled and sliced into rings

If you roll the liver in flour before cooking, the sauce will end up lovely and thick. And for the best flavour, remember not to overcook, to keep the liver pink. The cider in the onion ring batter just adds something a little bit fun and different.

If using a deep-fat fryer for the onion rings, heat the vegetable oil to 170°C (325°F). Alternatively, fill a deep, heavy-based frying pan to a depth of 2cm (¾in) with oil and use a sugar thermometer to check it has reached the correct temperature.

To make the batter, place the flour and salt in a bowl, then add the cider, a little at a time and stirring continuously, to form a smooth, thin batter.

To cook the liver, set a large frying pan over a high heat and add the butter. Season the liver with salt and pepper and dust lightly with a little flour. Add the liver to the pan, along with four of the sage leaves, frying in batches to ensure that the pan stays really hot and the liver is evenly browned all over, for maximum flavour. Fry for about 1½ minutes on each side, to ensure that the liver stays nice and pink in the middle, then transfer to a warmed plate and set aside.

Keeping the pan on a high heat, pour in the Madeira and the stock and stir with a wooden spoon to deglaze, loosening and incorporating any sediment from the bottom of the pan, then reduce the liquid by three-quarters.

To cook the onion rings, dip them and the remaining eight sage leaves in the batter and deep-fry in the hot oil. After about 1–2 minutes, remove from the oil with a slotted spoon and place on kitchen paper to dry, then sprinkle with salt.

Place the liver on plates, spoon over the sauce and add a pile of onion rings and fried sage on top. Serve either plain or with mash or a herby salad with a few capers mixed in.

Roasted grouse with potato, celeriac and parsnip rosti

Serves 4

4 grouse
2 onions, peeled and roughly chopped
1 tbsp olive oil
50ml (2fl oz) Marsala or other sweet dessert wine
200ml (7fl oz) red wine
1 sprig of thyme, leaves only
600ml (1 pint) beef or Chicken Stock (see page 216)
25g (1oz) butter

For the rosti
200g (7oz) celeriac
2 parsnips
2 medium baking potatoes
2 sprigs of thyme, leaves only
4 tbsp thick crème fraîche
2 egg yolks
3 tbsp olive oil
50g (2oz) butter
Salt and black pepper

I've been lucky enough to go grouse shooting up in Scotland. Or rather, the grouse were lucky, as I couldn't hit a barn door. It's a good job my butcher has grouse in stock, otherwise I'd never make this dish. The season runs from the start of August to the start of December and so this is the ideal autumnal game recipe.

Preheat the oven to 200°C (400°F), Gas 6.

Season the grouse well with salt and pepper and put the onions inside the cavity of each bird. Set a roasting tin on the hob over a high heat, add the olive oil to the tin, along with the grouse, and fry on all sides to seal and brown. Transfer to the oven and cook for 20 minutes. Baste the grouse from time to time with the oil while it is cooking.

Meanwhile, peel and grate the celeriac, parsnip and potato. Wrap in a clean tea towel and squeeze to get rid of any excess water, then tip into a large bowl, along with the thyme, crème fraîche and egg yolks. Mix well and season with salt and pepper, then divide the vegetable mixture into heaps of about 2 tablespoons and shape into 7.5cm (3in) patties of about 2cm (¾in) in height.

Add the olive oil and the butter to a non-stick frying pan set over a medium–high heat and, when the butter has melted, add the vegetable patties to the pan. Cook slowly, turning over after 3–4 minutes and cooking for the same amount of time on the other side.

Continued overleaf …

Remove the grouse from the oven and allow to rest. Pour away the fat and set the tin on the hob over a medium heat. Pour in the Marsala, the red wine and the thyme, and stir with a wooden spoon to deglaze, loosening and incorporating any sediment from the base of the tin. Add the stock, bring to the boil, reduce the heat and simmer to reduce the liquid by two-thirds. Stir in the butter and season, to taste, with salt and pepper.

Place one grouse on each plate, spoon over the sauce and serve with the rosti on the side.

Roast duck breast with sherry vinegar plums

Serves 4

8 tbsp runny honey

4 sprigs of thyme

4 large duck breasts, bone removed, ready for roasting

1 tsp olive oil

12 plums, cut into quarters and stones removed

25g (1oz) butter

2 star anise

2 cinnamon sticks

200ml (7fl oz) sherry vinegar

Salt and black pepper

Plums and cherries go very well with duck, their sweet sharpness cutting through the fattiness of the meat. Sherry vinegar has a similar effect, and really adds to the overall taste of this dish.

Preheat the oven to 200°C (400°C), Gas 6.

Set a frying pan over a high heat, add the honey and thyme, place the duck breasts in the pan, fat side down, and season with salt and pepper. Fry on both sides to seal and brown and, once well coloured, remove from the pan and place on a baking tray. Put in the oven and roast for 12 minutes, basting from time to time.

While the duck breasts are cooking, set another frying pan over a high heat and add the olive oil. Place the plums in the pan and sauté for 1 minute, then add the butter, star anise and cinnamon sticks and continue to cook, stirring from time to time, for 5 minutes. Just as the plums are starting to soften, pour in the sherry vinegar and stir with a wooden spoon to deglaze, loosening and incorporating any sediment from the base of the pan.

Remove the duck breasts from the oven and allow to rest before slicing into pieces to serve. Season the plums with salt and pepper, to taste, and spoon on to plates, placing slices of duck alongside.

Rabbit casserole with white wine and grapes

Serves 4

1 rabbit, cut into portions
20g (¾oz) flour, for dusting
1 tbsp olive oil
110g (4oz) baby shallots, peeled but left whole
200ml (7fl oz) white wine
1 clove of garlic, peeled and roughly chopped
3 sprigs of thyme
500ml (18fl oz) Chicken Stock (see page 216)
150g (5oz) seedless white grapes
Salt and black pepper

Rabbit tastes a bit like chicken, and is now widely farmed in the UK. It can be cooked in much the same way as chicken, although the legs are more substantial so require a longer cooking time. Serve with a crisp green salad or some sauté potatoes.

Preheat the oven to 170°C (325°F), Gas 3.

Coat the rabbit pieces in a light dusting of flour and season well with salt and pepper. Set a deep ovenproof pan with a tight-fitting lid over a high heat, add the olive oil and fry the rabbit in batches to seal and brown on all sides. Once each batch is sealed, remove from the pan and put on a plate while you fry the remaining meat.

Once all the meat has been sealed and transferred to the plate, add the shallots to the pan and fry all over to brown them. Return the rabbit to the pan, then add the wine and deglaze the pan using a wooden spoon, loosening and incorporating any sediment from the bottom of the pan. Add the garlic, the thyme sprigs and the stock, then bring to the boil, cover with the lid and place into the oven.

After 20 minutes, remove from the oven, add the grapes and place back into the oven for a further 15 minutes. Remove from the oven, season with salt and pepper and serve.

Venison with parsnip purée and roast beets

Serves 4

300g (11oz) fresh baby beetroot
1 tbsp olive oil
900g (2lb) loin of venison
2 sprigs of thyme, leaves only
3 parsnips, peeled and roughly chopped
110ml (4fl oz) milk
Caster sugar, to taste
200ml (7fl oz) double cream
1 tbsp balsamic vinegar
Salt and black pepper

The word 'venison' was once used to refer to the meat of any animal killed by hunting, but now it generally means deer meat. My favourite is the wild roe deer as it has the strongest flavour.

Place the beetroot in a large saucepan of cold water, add a good pinch of salt, bring to the boil and cook for 30 minutes, or until tender. Allow to cool and then peel and set aside.

Preheat the oven to 200°C (400°F), Gas 6. Set a non-stick ovenproof pan over a high heat and add the oil. While it is heating, season the venison and rub with thyme leaves, then place in the hot pan and fry on both sides to brown and seal. Cut each beetroot into six pieces and add to the pan with the venison. Transfer to the oven for 8 minutes to cook.

Place the parsnips in a large saucepan with 300ml (11fl oz) water and the milk. Season with salt and sugar and bring to the boil. Reduce the heat and simmer for 10–12 minutes, or until tender. Drain well, retaining the cooking liquid, then place the parsnips in a food processor with a little of the liquid and blend to a purée. Alternatively, blitz using a hand-held blender. Transfer to a clean saucepan with enough cream to make a smooth, creamy purée, set over a gentle heat and allow to warm through. Season with more salt and sugar.

Remove the venison from the oven and the pan, transfer to a chopping board and allow to rest for 5–8 minutes, then slice the meat. Place the pan back on the hob over a high heat, add a dash of balsamic vinegar, season with salt and pepper and stir in with the beetroot in the pan. Remove from the heat. To serve, spoon the parsnip purée on to plates, arrange the venison on the top and a pile of beetroot on the side.

Pheasant breasts with onion purée and sautéed greens

Serves 4

20g (¾oz) unsalted butter
1 tbsp olive oil
4 x pheasant breasts, on the bone
2 sprigs of thyme
50ml (2fl oz) port
200ml (7fl oz) beef stock

For the onion purée
1 tbsp olive oil
3 onions, peeled and thinly sliced
300ml (11fl oz) double cream
Salt and black pepper

For the sautéed greens
25g (1oz) butter
½ clove of garlic, peeled and crushed
2 bunches of greens (such as savoy or pointed cabbage), sliced into 1cm (½in) lengths

Pheasants are so cheap at this time of year, and can be bought from the farmers' market or your butcher. Cook until just pink and serve with this strongly-flavoured onion purée for a nice change from mash. The greens can be cooked in a pan with water and a bit of butter – the butter prevents them from overcooking and really adds to the flavour.

To make the purée, set a frying pan over a medium heat, add the olive oil and the onions and allow these to sweat, without browning, for 5 minutes. Add the cream and simmer for 15 minutes until thick in consistency. Place in a blender, or use a hand-held blender, and purée until smooth, season with salt and pepper and set aside.

Preheat the oven to 240°C (475°F), Gas 9. Set an ovenproof pan or roasting tin over a hob set to a high heat, add the butter and olive oil. When the butter has melted, add the pheasant breasts and cook on both sides to seal and brown, then add the thyme.

Place in the oven, immediately reducing the temperature to 200°C (400°F), Gas 6. Roast for 12–15 minutes, depending on how well done you like your pheasant. Allow to rest for 5–8 minutes in the warm tin.

While the pheasant is cooking, set a frying pan over a medium heat, add the butter and garlic, followed by the greens, and sauté for 30 seconds. Pour over 75ml (3fl oz) water, season with salt and plenty of pepper and sauté well together. The greens should cook in 3–4 minutes.

Remove the pheasant breasts from the pan and set aside, then place the pan over a medium heat. Add the port to the pan and stir with a wooden spoon to deglaze, loosening and incorporating any sediment from the bottom of the pan. Reduce the liquid by two-thirds, add the stock, raise the heat and simmer for 3–4 minutes. Season with salt and pepper.

Carve the pheasant breasts from the bone, arrange on plates, pour over the sauce and serve with a pile of greens and a spoonful of onion purée, reheated if necessary, on the side.

Pork escalopes with wild mushrooms, juniper and mash

Serves 4

4 large Estima potatoes, peeled and cut into quarters
110g (4oz) butter
175ml (6fl oz) double cream
1 tbsp olive oil
4 x 175–225g (6–8oz) escalopes of pork
2 shallots, peeled and sliced into fine rings
4 juniper berries, crushed
400g (14oz) mixed wild mushrooms (such as chanterelles, trompettes, girolles), wiped clean
2 tbsp sherry
1 clove of garlic, peeled and finely chopped
2 tbsp chopped flat-leaf parsley
Salt and black pepper

For too long we have been breeding pork to be as lean as a catwalk model, but fat is important to the taste, so make sure the pork you buy has a generous layer. For some of the best pork suppliers, see the Supplier list on page 219. Good, free-range pork, like any properly produced food, may cost that little bit extra, but it's definitely worthwhile as the flavour is far superior.

Place the potato quarters in a large saucepan, fill with water, add a pinch of salt and bring to the boil. Cook for 20 minutes or so until softened, then drain and return to the pan. Mash with half the butter and two-thirds of the cream, season with salt and pepper and keep warm in the pan.

Meanwhile, set a frying pan over a high heat and add the oil and half the remaining butter. Season the pork well with salt and pepper and, when the butter has melted, add the pork to the pan. Fry for 3–4 minutes on both sides, then remove from the pan and set aside.

Set the pan back over the heat, add the remaining butter and, when it has melted, tip in the shallots, juniper berries and mushrooms. Sauté together quickly, add the sherry and cook for 1–2 minutes to allow the alcohol to evaporate off. Alternatively, burn off the alcohol by carefully lighting it with a match. Add the garlic and the remaining cream, if you wish, and cook for 2 minutes.

Spoon the mash on to each plate, place a pork escalope alongside, add the wild mushroom mixture and scatter over the parsley. Season with salt and pepper and serve.

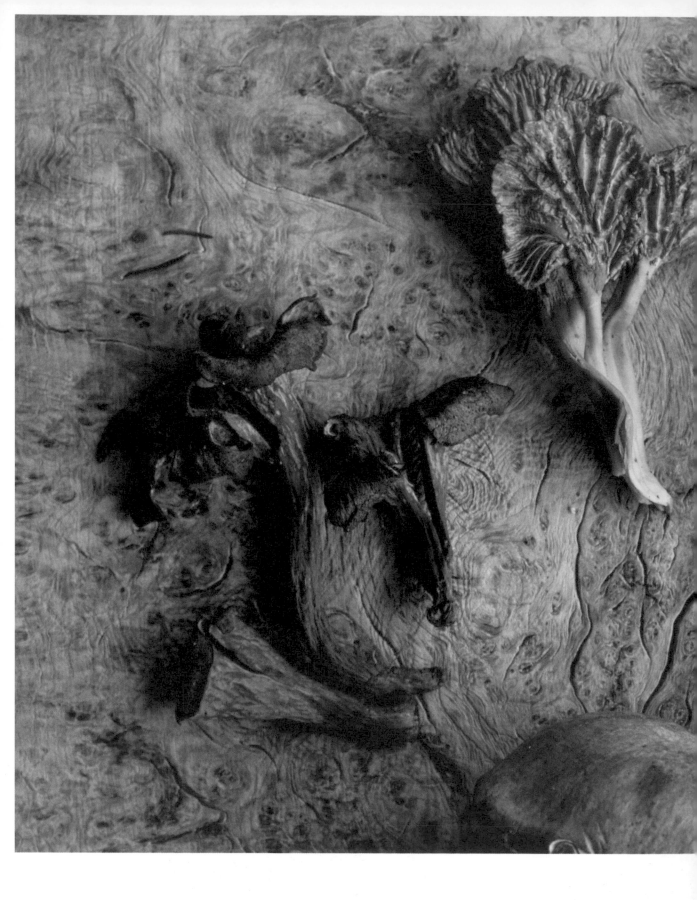

Swiss-style hazelnut meringues with coffee cream

Serves 4–6

6 medium egg whites
225g (8oz) caster sugar
**125g (4½oz) dark soft
    brown sugar**
**75g (3oz) dark
    chocolate (50–70%
    cocoa solids)**
**40g (1½oz) shelled
    hazelnuts, skinned
    (see page 30) and
    roughly chopped**
**150ml (5fl oz) double
    cream**
3 tbsp icing sugar
**4 tbsp very strong cold
    coffee**

This is an unusual way to make meringue which I learned from a Swiss guy I once met. When served with this coffee cream, I can guarantee you will want more than one of these.

Bring a medium-sized saucepan to a simmer and find a pyrex bowl that fits comfortably on top without touching the water.

Put the egg whites and both types of sugar into the bowl, sit it above the simmering water and stir gently for 6–8 minutes, or until the sugar dissolves. Take care not to overheat the bowl, or the egg whites will begin to cook. Once the sugar has dissolved, pour the contents of the bowl into a food processor and whisk on high speed for 6–8 minutes until light and fluffy. Alternatively, use an electric beater.

Preheat the oven to 110°C (225°F), Gas ¼ (or lowest setting). Grate half the chocolate and fold into the fluffy meringue mixture. Line a baking sheet with parchment paper and spoon the meringue on to it in small dollops, leaving enough space for them to double in size while cooking.

Sprinkle three-quarters of the hazelnuts over the top and bake in the oven for 1¼–1½ hours until set. Check this by lifting the meringues gently and lightly tapping the bases. If they come away easily from the parchment paper and make a hollow sound, they are ready. Allow to cool.

Meanwhile, softly whip the cream with the icing sugar, then stir in the coffee to make a marbled pattern. Serve meringues on plates with a dollop of marbled cream and the rest of the grated chocolate and chopped nuts sprinkled over the top.

Welsh cakes with poached pears

Serves 4
(Makes 12–15 cakes)

4 small pears, peeled
    but left whole
1 lemon, zested and cut
    in half
275g (10oz) caster
    sugar
225g (8oz) self-raising
    flour, sifted, plus
    extra for dusting
½ tsp mixed spice
Pinch of salt
110g (4oz) butter, cut
    into pieces
75g (3oz) sultanas
1 large egg, beaten
Dash of milk (optional)
Lard or vegetable oil,
    for greasing
Vanilla ice cream, to
    serve

Also known as bakestones, my folks eat these little cakes at teatime but I like them as a pud. The instructions below are for making the cakes by hand as this gives them a much nicer texture.

Put the pears in a large saucepan of water. Squeeze in the juice from the lemon and drop in the lemon halves, keeping the zest for later. Add 200g (7oz) of the caster sugar, bring to the boil, then reduce the heat and simmer for 15–20 minutes, until the pears are soft but still whole. Remove from the heat and leave in the pan to cool.

To make the Welsh cakes, place the flour, mixed spice and salt into a large bowl and stir in the remaining caster sugar and the lemon zest. Rub in the butter with your fingertips until the mixture resembles breadcrumbs – this should take about 5 minutes. Add the sultanas and mix well, then stir in the beaten egg and use your hands to bring the mixture together to form a dough. If it is too dry, add a dash of milk.

Place the dough on a lightly floured surface and roll out to a thickness of about 0.5cm (¼in). Use a 10cm (4in) plain, round cutter to cut the dough into cakes, then re-roll the remaining dough and repeat. Lightly grease a griddle or heavy-based frying pan with lard or vegetable oil. Set over a low heat and lightly cook the cakes (in batches, if necessary) for 1–2 minutes on each side or until golden brown. Remove from the pan and cool on a wire rack.

When ready to serve, remove the pears from the saucepan and dry on kitchen paper. Serve the Welsh cakes and pears with scoops of vanilla ice cream.

Baked custard tart with mulled spiced plums

Serves 6–8

25g (1oz) butter, for greasing
250g (9oz) ready-made sweet shortcrust pasty
Flour, for dusting
800ml (29fl oz) double cream
1 vanilla pod, cut in two
10 medium egg yolks
2 medium whole eggs
200g (7oz) caster sugar

For the mulled spiced plums
8–10 dark-skinned plums
4 tbsp caster sugar
50g (2oz) butter
110ml (4fl oz) red wine
1 cinnamon stick
½ tsp freshly grated nutmeg
2 cloves
1 bay leaf
2 star anise

The real secret to making custard and set-egg tarts is to bake them at a low temperature so that the custard doesn't split or curdle.

Preheat the oven to 180°C (350°F), Gas 4. Grease a 30cm x 4cm (12in x 1½in) flan dish.

Roll out the pastry on a lightly floured work surface to a size slightly larger than the flan dish. Lay the pastry over the dish and press it gently into the base and sides, leaving any excess pastry hanging over the edge until after it is cooked. Line with greaseproof paper and fill with uncooked rice or baking beans and leave to rest in the fridge for 20–30 minutes.

Remove from the fridge and bake 'blind' for 12–15 minutes. Once the pastry shell is cooked, remove from the oven and take out the greaseproof paper and rice or baking beans.

Turn the oven temperature down to 130°C (250°F), Gas ½.

To make the filling, pour the cream into a large saucepan, scrape the seeds from the vanilla pod into the pan and add the pod. Bring to the boil, then set aside to infuse. Meanwhile mix the egg yolks, whole egg and sugar together in a large bowl. Stir in the cream mixture a little at a time, then pass through a sieve into another bowl or a measuring jug.

Place the tart base on a baking sheet and put it in the oven, then pull out the oven shelf a little (as it is easier to fill the tart case while it's in the oven). Fill the tart case full to the brim with the custard mixture and carefully slide the shelf back in. Cook for about 45 minutes to 1 hour. You can tell when it's cooked by shaking the tray a little to see if the custard is set.

While the tart is cooking, remove the stones from the plums and cut into quarters. Set a frying pan over a high heat and add the sugar and butter. When the butter has melted and is bubbling, add the plums, wine and spices. Simmer for 10 minutes until the juice has reduced to a syrup, then remove from the heat and allow to cool a little.

Take the tart from the oven and allow to cool to room temperature before trimming off any overhanging crust, cutting the tart into slices and serving with the warm spiced plums.

Damson clafoutis

Serves 4–6

**25g (1oz) butter,
    softened**
**30g (1¼oz) flour, for
    dusting**
50g (2oz) caster sugar
**50ml (2fl oz) white
    wine**
Juice of 1 lemon
**500g (1lb 2oz) fresh
    damsons or plums,
    cut in half and
    stones removed**
Icing sugar, for dusting
**Vanilla ice cream, to
    serve**

For the batter
125ml (4½fl oz) milk
**1 vanilla pod, cut in
    two**
**150ml (5fl oz)
    whipping cream**
75ml (3fl oz) brandy
5 eggs
**125g (4½oz) caster
    sugar**
Pinch of salt
40g (1½oz) plain flour

A clafoutis is a dessert in which fresh fruit is baked in a custard-like batter. The damson season runs from August through to October. The fruit is a small variety of plum, but can be quite sour, so is much better when cooked. They are also excellent for jellies and jams and very good stewed for serving with meats like roast duck or game.

Preheat the oven to 180°C (350°F), Gas 4. Spread the softened butter all over the inside of a 30cm x 20cm (12in x 8in) ovenproof dish, sprinkle with a little flour and set aside.

Set a non-stick frying pan over a medium heat and add the sugar, wine and lemon juice. Then add the damson halves, cover with a piece of greaseproof paper and cook gently for 3–4 minutes. Turn the halves over and continue cooking for a few more minutes, then remove from the heat and allow to cool in the pan.

Meanwhile, make the batter. Pour the milk into a saucepan, scrape in the seeds from the vanilla pod, add the pod itself and bring to the boil. Remove from the heat and allow to cool slightly, then stir in the cream and brandy. In a large bowl, whisk the eggs, sugar and salt until the mixture doubles in volume. Fold in the flour, and then the milk mixture.

Arrange the damson halves, cut side up, in the bottom of the buttered dish, and pour over the batter. Place in the oven and bake for 30–35 minutes, until just set. Remove from the oven, allow to cool until slightly warm, then dust with icing sugar and serve with the ice cream.

Pistachio coffee cake

Serves 4

**225g (8oz) butter,
softened, plus extra
for greasing**
225g (8oz) caster sugar
4 large eggs
**3 tbsp strong cold
coffee**
**75g (3oz) shelled
pistachio nuts, very
finely chopped**
**250g (9oz) self-raising
flour, sifted**
**25g (1oz) icing sugar,
for dusting**

For the filling
**300ml (11fl oz) double
cream**
2 tbsp icing sugar
**110g (4oz) shelled
pistachios, roughly
chopped**

*Everybody loves cake, including me! My gran and auntie were
masters at baking, so I've nicked their best recipe and added a few
more ingredients. Cheers, ladies.*

Preheat the oven to 190°C (375°F), Gas 5. Grease a deep,
23cm (9in) diameter spring-form or loose-bottomed cake tin.

Place the butter and sugar in a large bowl and whisk until
light and fluffy, add the eggs, one at a time, beating between
each addition until well incorporated. Be careful not to add
them too quickly or the mixture will tend to curdle.

Add the coffee and chopped nuts and mix well, then carefully
fold in the flour. Pour the mixture straight away into the cake
tin, transfer to the oven and bake for 20–25 minutes, or until
golden brown and well risen. Remove from the oven and
allow to cool for 30 minutes in the tin before transferring to
a wire rack to finish cooling.

For the filling, pour the cream into a bowl and whisk until it
forms soft peaks, add the icing sugar and pistachios and fold
gently with a spatula until the mixture forms firm peaks,
being careful not to over-mix.

To finish the cake, carefully cut it in half horizontally with a
bread knife and place the bottom half on to a serving plate.
Spread the pistachio cream over the bottom half of the cake,
then cover with the other half. Top with a dusting of icing
sugar and serve.

Sloe jam

Makes 1 litre (2½ pints)

1.5kg (3lb 4oz) sloes
300g (11oz) Golden
    Delicious apples
1.3kg (3lb) granulated
    sugar
1 vanilla pod, cut in
    two

In Autumn, the hedgerows come alive with free food, so get outside and start collecting! It's amazing how much fruit you end up with. Stored properly, this jam should keep for a year, at least.

First, place the sloes in the freezer for several hours, or ideally overnight, to freeze them through. Remove from the freezer, place in a large bowl, pour over boiling water, to cover, and leave to cool.

Core and peel the apples and cut into 1cm (½in) cubes, then drain the sloes and place with the apples in a large saucepan set over a medium heat. Add 100ml (4fl oz) of water and simmer gently for 15 minutes, or until soft.

Add the sugar and vanilla pod, together with the seeds scraped from the pod, and, once the sugar has dissolved, turn up the heat and reduce by about a third. To test whether the setting point has been reached, pour a little of the jam on to a cold plate, allow to cool briefly in the fridge, then see if your finger, drawn through the centre, leaves a clear line. If not, return to the pan to the heat and cook the jam for a few more minutes, then repeat the setting test.

When the setting point has been reached, pass the jam through a sieve, set over a large, clean bowl, to remove the stones.

Preheat the oven to 150°C (300°F), Gas 2. To sterilise jars for the jam, wash them in hot soapy water, rinse with hot water – without touching the inside of the jars – and place in the oven for 2–3 minutes. Remove and allow to cool before filling with the jam. Cover each with a disc of waxed paper, waxed side down, and seal with an airtight lid. Label and store in a cool, dark place.

Winter

**Shallots • Parsnips • Celeriac • Brussels sprouts
Leeks • Potatoes • Cabbage • Chestnuts • Quinces
Cranberries • Beef • Turkey • Mussels • Scallops**

'Tis the season to be jolly, especially if you're a keen cook. The garden may seem bare, but take a closer look and you'll find there are still delights to be tasted, from leeks and winter greens to parsnips and celeriac. Root veg, beetroot and artichokes go perfectly alongside game, beef and turkey. Enjoy delicious winter seafood such as mussels and scallops. And don't forget those apples and pears which are stored for use, or there's the more exotic quince – perfect for use in jellies and tarts.

Chunky vegetable soup with cheesy herb toasts

Serves 4
Vegetarian

2 cloves of garlic
2 shallots
1 medium leek
1 medium potato
1 large parsnip
1 large carrot
1 butternut squash
25g (1oz) butter
110ml (4fl oz) white wine
1 litre (1¾ pints) Vegetable Stock (see page 218)
125g (4½oz) mature Cheddar cheese, grated
25g flat-leaf parsley, chopped
25g chives, chopped
1 ciabatta loaf
Salt and black pepper

Many people think of soups and stews as a way to use up leftovers and old veg. In fact, the best possible soups are those that use the freshest ingredients. Be careful not to overcook the vegetables for this dish as it will spoil the flavours.

Peel and crush the garlic and peel all the other vegetables and cut into 1cm (½in) cubes. Melt the butter in a large, heavy-based saucepan set over a high heat, add all the vegetables and sauté for 2 minutes without browning.

Pour in the wine and stock, bring to the boil, reduce the heat and simmer for 6–8 minutes until the vegetables are just softened – it's important not to overcook them.

Place the grated cheese in a bowl, add half of the herbs and mix together.

Preheat the grill to medium. Slice the bread, place under the grill and toast both sides. Remove from the grill, top with the herb and cheese mixture and place under the grill again to melt the cheese.

Season the soup well with salt and pepper, add the remaining chopped herbs and serve with the cheese and herb toasts.

Leek and potato soup with smoked salmon and poached eggs

Serves 4

50g (2oz) butter
2 cloves of garlic, peeled and roughly chopped
1 shallot, peeled and roughly chopped
1 large baking potato, peeled and chopped into small cubes
1 medium leek, sliced
1 chicken stock cube, crumbled
110ml (4fl oz) white wine
125ml (4½fl oz) double cream
5g (¼oz) flat-leaf parsley
4 eggs
1 tbsp white wine vinegar
200g (7oz) smoked salmon, cut into thin strips
Salt and black pepper

A classic soup, but with a hidden surprise. Poached eggs are great in soups as they're like a hidden gem waiting to be discovered – the pearl in the oyster. For this dish, you could replace the smoked salmon with smoked haddock for a slightly different flavour.

Melt the butter in a large, heavy-based saucepan set over a high heat, add all the prepared vegetables and sauté for 2 minutes without browning.

Place the stock cube and wine in another saucepan, add 600ml (1 pint) hot water and bring to the boil, then add to the potato mixture and simmer for 2 minutes. Add the cream and most of the parsley, keeping a little back for a garnish, then season with salt and pepper and purée in a blender, or using a hand-held blender, until smooth.

In a separate saucepan bring some water to the boil, then crack the eggs into four separate cups. When the water is boiling rapidly, add a drizzle of vinegar, stir the water to make a whirlpool, then carefully drop the eggs in one by one. Cook for 2 minutes, or longer if you prefer the yolks to be less runny. Using a slotted spoon, remove from the water and put onto a warmed plate, and set aside.

Bring the creamed soup to the boil, pour into bowls and place a poached egg in the centre of each, along with a sprinkling of the smoked salmon. Chop the remaining parsley and sprinkle over the soup to serve.

Onion soup with Lincolnshire Poacher

Serves 4
Vegetarian

25g (1oz) butter
6 white onions, peeled
  and thinly sliced
2 cloves of garlic,
  peeled and crushed
8g (⅓oz) plain flour
175ml (6fl oz) white
  wine
600ml (1 pint)
  Vegetable or Chicken
  Stock (see pages 218
  and 216)
200ml (7fl oz) double
  cream
110g (4oz) Lincolnshire
  Poacher cheese (or
  mature Cheddar),
  grated
20g (¾oz) chives,
  chopped
Salt and black pepper

Onions have been one of the most successful and easiest crops I've grown in my vegetable plot so far. This soup combines the best of my garden with my favourite cheese, Lincolnshire Poacher. Made by Simon and Tim Jones from Alford, it is an amazing, unpasteurised cow's milk cheese with a smooth nutty taste, quite like a rich Cheddar.

Melt the butter in a large heavy-based saucepan set over a medium heat, add the onions and garlic and sauté for 2 minutes without browning. Stir in the flour, then pour in the wine and stock. Bring to the boil, then reduce the heat and simmer for 6–8 minutes.

Add the cream and purée with a hand-held blender or in a blender. Return to the pan and heat through gently, then season well with salt and pepper and serve in bowls with the cheese and chives sprinkled over the top.

Gnocchi with winter pesto

Serves 4
Vegetarian

1kg (2lb 2oz) floury
   potatoes, all about the
   same size
1 egg
300g (11oz) strong
   white flour, plus extra
   for dusting
Semolina, for dusting
   (optional, instead of
   flour)
Salt and black pepper

For the pesto
150ml (5fl oz) extra-
   virgin olive oil, plus
   extra for frying
1 shallot, peeled and
   finely chopped
2 cloves of garlic,
   peeled and finely
   chopped
300g (11oz) watercress
300g (11oz) rocket
110g (4oz) lamb's or
   corn lettuce
150g (5oz) Parmesan
   cheese, freshly grated

I learned the art of making gnocchi in a restaurant in Rome, so this simple recipe is as authentic as it gets. The pesto is made from cooked winter salad leaves, and the use of watercress and rocket gives it a wonderful peppery taste. Because salads grow all year round, this pesto can be adapted for all seasons – just use whichever leaves are available.

To make the gnocchi, place the unpeeled potatoes in a large saucepan of salted water and bring to the boil. Simmer for 20–30 minutes until they are cooked but not falling apart. Drain and cool slightly before removing the skins and mashing well in the pan. Set aside to allow to cool.

Once cool, add the egg, 1 teaspoon of salt and the flour and mix well. On a work surface lightly dusted with flour or, preferably, semolina, roll out the dough into a long, thin sausage and cut into small discs about 2cm (¾in) in diameter. Gently soften the edges with your fingers so the discs look like small dumplings. Transfer to a plate and place in the fridge for a minimum of 30 minutes (they can be left overnight).

To make the pesto, set a frying pan over a medium heat, add a little olive oil and sauté the shallot and garlic for 1 minute. Add half of each of the different salad leaves, turn up the heat and wilt the leaves for 2 minutes. Place in a blender with two-thirds of the olive oil and half the Parmesan and blend to a pesto. Transfer to a bowl and set aside.

Place a saucepan of water on the hob and bring to the boil with a good pinch of salt. Add the gnocchi and cook for 2 minutes – when cooked the gnocchi will rise to the surface. Using a slotted spoon, scoop out the gnocchi and drain well before frying.

Set a large, non-stick frying pan over a medium heat, pour in a little olive oil and add the gnocchi while they are still warm. Add the remaining salad leaves and sauté together for 2 minutes. Add the pesto, season with salt and pepper, stir well together and spoon on to plates. Top with the remaining Parmesan, drizzle with the remaining olive oil and serve.

Scallops with black pudding and apple purée

Serves 4

2 cooking apples
Juice of ½ lemon
12 slices of black pudding
1–3 tbsp olive oil
12 scallops, taken from the shell, any roe removed
25g (1oz) butter
1 tbsp chopped flat-leaf parsley
Salt and black pepper

Hand-dived scallops are best for this recipe, if you can get them. Not only are they bigger, but they are better for the environment (as dredging can harm the seabed). I was always told by my gran that the best black pudding should have bits in it – bits that you can see – and should not be puréed. I know for a fact that she was right – it makes all the difference to the flavour.

Peel and core the apples, then cut into cubes and place them in a heavy-based saucepan with a lid. Add the lemon juice and a splash of water and gently bring to the boil with the lid on. Cook until tender then remove from the heat and purée in the pan with a hand-held blender. Set aside.

Set a large, non-stick frying pan over a medium heat. When it's hot, add the black pudding and allow to cook for 2–3 minutes before turning the slices over and cooking for a further 2–3 minutes, then remove from the pan and set aside on a warmed plate.

In the same pan, pour in 1 tablespoon of the olive oil and add the scallops, flat side down. Cook over a high heat for 1–2 minutes or until the edges of the scallops start to turn golden brown. Turn the scallops over, add the butter and allow it to melt, then remove from the heat and continue basting the scallops with the butter for another 1–2 minutes. Season with salt and pepper.

Spoon a dollop of apple purée on to each plate, then add three slices of black pudding. Place three scallops on top of the black pudding, sprinkle with parsley and drizzle with the remaining olive oil, if you wish.

Spicy mussels with coconut and lime

Serves 4

40g (1½oz) butter
1 onion, peeled and chopped
3 cloves of garlic, peeled and crushed
1 red chilli, deseeded and finely chopped
1 lemongrass stick
4 sprigs of thyme
1.3kg (3lb) mussels, washed and beards removed
250ml (9fl oz) white wine
110ml (4fl oz) double cream
400ml (14fl oz) coconut milk
50g (2oz) flat-leaf parsley, roughly chopped
Zest and juice of 1 lime
Salt and black pepper

Mussels work well with so many different flavours, from saffron to chilli to coconut. Here, the fresh combination of tastes provides a cheering tropical touch in the midst of winter. Make sure you clean the mussels well before using them and, once cooked, throw away any that haven't opened before you serve them.

Melt half the butter in a large, lidded saucepan set over a medium heat and sauté the onion, garlic, chilli, lemongrass and thyme for 1 minute, then add the mussels and stir well together. Pour in the wine, place the lid on the pan and cook for 4–5 minutes.

Add the rest of the butter to the pan, along with the cream and coconut milk, then season with salt and pepper. Sprinkle in the parsley and stir all the ingredients together. Add the lime zest and juice, then spoon the mussels into bowls, discard the lemongrass stick and pour the sauce left in the pan over the top of the mussels to serve.

Deep-fried cod cheeks in beer batter

Serves 4

**500g (1lb 2oz) cod
cheeks, membrane
removed, or fillets of
cod cut into bite-
sized pieces**
**3 cloves of garlic,
peeled and crushed**
**½ bunch of dill,
chopped**
**1.2 litres (2 pints)
vegetable oil, for
deep-frying**
**Tartar Sauce, to serve
(see page 215)**

For the batter
15g (½oz) fresh yeast
Pinch of salt
Pinch of caster sugar
200ml (7fl oz) beer
1 tsp cider vinegar
200g (7oz) plain flour

*Fish cheeks are rarely used in British cooking, and I'm not quite
sure why. Fish are often filleted at sea and the rest thrown back,
but if more people asked their fishmonger for the cheeks, then
fishermen would make an effort to keep them. Monkfish cheeks
are also excellent; bear in mind that the cheeks of any species have
a membrane that needs to be removed before cooking. You could
also use fillets of cod loin for this recipe.*

To make the batter, sprinkle the yeast, salt and sugar into a
large bowl. Pour over the beer and vinegar and whisk in the
flour. Leave to ferment for 15–20 minutes – it is ready to use
when the mixture starts to bubble.

If using a deep-fat fryer, heat the vegetable oil to 180°C
(350°F). Alternatively, fill a deep, heavy-based frying pan to
a depth of 2cm (¾in) with oil and use a sugar thermometer
to check that it has reached the correct temperature.

Cut each of the cod cheeks in half and place in a bowl. Add
the garlic and dill and toss together. Dip the cod cheeks into
the batter and fry in batches for 3–4 minutes until golden
brown. Remove with a slotted spoon and drain on kitchen
paper. Serve with Tartar Sauce.

Pigeon with fried green cabbage and almonds

Serves 4

50g (2oz) butter, cut into cubes

25g (1oz) flaked almonds

2 tbsp olive oil

2 shallots, peeled and sliced

2 cloves of garlic, peeled and crushed

2 sprigs of thyme

½ green cabbage, finely shredded

8 pigeon breasts

50ml (2fl oz) red wine vinegar

1 tsp chopped chives

Salt and black pepper

The common wood pigeon is the best type to eat and should be served pink. If roasting or grilling, cover it with bacon to keep it moist, else the meat can dry out very quickly.

Melt 15g (½oz) butter in a small frying pan set over a high heat, add the almonds and sauté for 2–3 minutes until lightly browned. As soon as they turn brown, remove the nuts from the pan to prevent them burning.

Pour half the olive oil into a heavy-based frying pan with a lid and fry the shallot over a medium heat but without browning. Add the garlic and thyme, then add the cabbage and mix in well. Season with salt and pepper and allow to cook slowly for 4–5 minutes with the lid on, then remove from the heat.

Drizzle the remaining olive oil into a non-stick frying pan set over a medium–high heat and season the pigeon breasts with salt and pepper. When the pan is hot, place the breasts in the pan, skin side down, and allow to cook for 3–4 minutes or until they start to turn golden brown, then turn over and cook for another 3–4 minutes.

Remove the pigeon breasts from the pan and set aside on a warmed plate to rest, then add the vinegar to the pan, still over the heat, and simmer to reduce by half. Add the remaining butter, remove the pan from the heat and whisk in the chives.

Sprinkle the toasted almonds over the cabbage in the pan. To serve, spoon on to plates and arrange the pigeon on top. Drizzle with the butter and chive sauce.

Roast turkey with Guinness glaze

Serves 6–8

**4.5kg (9¾lb) oven-
  ready turkey
3 tbsp olive oil
300ml (11fl oz)
  Guinness
110ml (4fl oz) runny
  honey
Salt and black pepper**

An unusual combination, yes, but Guinness is great to cook with and goes brilliantly with both chicken and turkey. The honey in this recipe causes the mixture to thicken while it is cooking. Baste the turkey frequently but don't make the gravy from the pan juices. Serve with carrots, parsnips and roast potatoes.

Preheat the oven to 180°C (350°F), Gas 4.

Place the turkey in a roasting tin and drizzle with the olive oil. Season well with salt and pepper, then place in the oven and roast for 3 hours and 20 minutes (or if cooking a turkey of a different size, allow about 20 minutes per lb), until the juices run clear when the thickest part of the leg is pierced with a knife. Check on the turkey from time to time – if it looks like it is colouring too much, remove from the oven and cover with foil, then return for the remaining cooking time.

Halfway though the cooking, mix the beer and honey together and brush the mixture over the turkey, then place the bird back in the oven. Baste the turkey with the pan juices every 15 minutes until cooked, to glaze the turkey. Remove from the oven, cover with foil and leave to stand for 15 minutes before carving.

Breaded turkey with spinach, walnuts and honeyed parsnips

Serves 4

75g (3oz) plain flour
2 eggs
300g (11oz) dried breadcrumbs, such as Japanese panko
4 x 200g (7oz) turkey escalopes
75g (3oz) butter
4 tbsp runny honey
4 parsnips, peeled and cut into batons
50g (2oz) walnut halves
60g (2½oz) baby spinach leaves
Salt and black pepper

When preparing escalopes that are coated in breadcrumbs, you will need to cook them in plenty of butter. This adds colour and flavour but, above all, is essential for crisping up the breadcrumbs.

Pour the flour on to a plate, crack the eggs into a bowl, beating them slightly, and place the breadcrumbs on another plate. Season the turkey escalopes with salt and pepper and dip first into the flour, dusting off any excess, then into the egg and finally into the breadcrumbs, coating all over.

Melt half the butter in a frying pan set over a medium heat. Add the honey, parsnips and 90ml (3½fl oz) water and simmer for 6–8 minutes, or until the liquid evaporates and a glaze is left in the pan. Add the walnuts and spinach, mix together with the parsnips until coated in the glaze and season well with salt and pepper.

While the parsnips are still simmering (before the spinach is added), set a non-stick frying pan over a medium heat, add the remaining butter and, when it is foaming, add the escalopes and cook until golden brown on one side before turning over. These should take only 4–5 minutes in total to cook. Remove from the pan and serve with the warm spinach and parsnips on the side.

Beef fillet with bacon, cep purée and Jerusalem artichokes

Serves 4

4 x 225g (8oz) fillets
 of beef
1 tbsp olive oil
50g (2oz) butter
300g (11oz) Jerusalem
 artichokes
8 slices of dry-cured
 back bacon, cut into
 lardons
4 tbsp chopped flat-
 leaf parsley
Salt and black pepper

For the cep purée
15g (½oz) butter
1 shallot, chopped
1 clove of garlic, peeled
 and chopped
25g (1oz) ceps,
 chopped
110g (4oz) button
 mushrooms, chopped
50ml (2fl oz) white
 wine
110ml (4fl oz) double
 cream

The cep purée makes this dish sound a bit posh and 'cheffy', but it's really delicious and fresh cep mushrooms are easy to get hold of early in winter. If you can't find them, you can use dried ceps, or even frozen ones instead.

To make the cep purée, melt the butter in a frying pan set over a medium heat and add the shallot and garlic. Sauté for 1 minute, then add the mushrooms and sauté for 3 minutes. Add the wine and cream and simmer for 5 minutes until thickened. Place in a blender and mix to a purée, or purée with a hand-held blender, then season with salt and pepper and set aside.

To cook the steaks, first season with salt and pepper, then add to a hot frying pan set over a high heat. Brown well on one side before turning over. Add the olive oil and half the butter and cook to your liking – 2–3 minutes for rare, 5 minutes for medium, 7–8 for well done – basting all the time.

While the fillets are cooking, peel and thinly slice the Jerusalem artichokes. Melt the remaining butter in a non-stick frying pan and fry the bacon until crisp, then remove from the pan and dry on kitchen paper. Tip in the artichokes and sauté for 5 minutes, or until they are golden brown, then return the bacon to the pan.

Add the parsley and season well with salt and pepper. To serve, place the artichoke and bacon mixture in a pile in the middle of each plate, with a steak on top, the pan juices spooned over and the cep purée, reheated if needed, on the side.

Braised oxtail with beer and red wine

Serves 4

1.6kg (3½lb) oxtail, cut into pieces
40g (1½oz) plain flour
4 tbsp olive oil
1 x 750ml bottle good-quality red wine (such as burgundy)
1 x 350ml bottle Guinness
4 sprigs of thyme
10 shallots, peeled and left whole
2 cloves of garlic, peeled and crushed
8 tbsp chopped flat-leaf parsley (optional)
25g (1oz) butter
Salt and black pepper

Brown the meat well to begin with and then cook this dish for as long as possible. You could cook it in a slow cooker, if you liked, or overnight in the oven at a very low temperature. Baste from time to time while it cooks and serve with a big pile of creamy mash on the side.

Preheat the oven to 150°C (300°F), Gas 2.

Dust the oxtail with the flour and season well with salt and pepper. Pour the olive oil into a large casserole dish set over high heat. Add the oxtail to the hot casserole dish in small batches and quickly seal on all sides, cooking until the meat begins to brown. Remove each batch from the casserole, transfer to a plate and repeat with the remaining pieces.

Once all the batches of meat have been sealed, return all of the oxtail to the casserole, then pour in the wine and beer. Add the thyme, shallots and the garlic, bring to the boil, cover with the lid and cook gently in the oven for 4–5 hours, or until the meat is so tender that it is falling apart.

When the cooking time is up, remove the casserole from the oven, add the chopped parsley and the butter, season well with salt and pepper and serve.

Beef and shallot hotpot

Serves 4–6

900g (2lb) stewing beef, cut into 4cm (1½in) chunks
1 tbsp vegetable oil
75–110g (3–4oz) butter
14 shallots, peeled and left whole
1 tbsp plain flour
200ml (7fl oz) red wine
600ml (1 pint) beef stock
2 sprigs of thyme
900g (2lb) potatoes, peeled and cut into 3–4mm (⅛in) slices
Sea salt and black pepper

I love this traditional British dish, especially on a cold winter's day. Slow cooking has had a comeback recently and rightly so, as it's my favourite form of cooking, with brilliantly rich flavours. Serve with well-buttered carrots or winter greens such as cabbage.

Preheat the oven to 170°C (325°F), Gas 3. Trim the beef of any excess fat and pat dry with kitchen paper.

Place the oil and about a third of the butter in a large, heavy-based frying pan set over a high heat. When the butter is bubbling, add the beef, 2–3 pieces at a time, and fry until browned on all sides. Remove each batch from the pan as it is cooked and place in a large casserole or ovenproof dish.

Add the shallots to the frying pan, reducing the heat to medium, adding a little more butter if necessary. Fry for about 5 minutes until lightly browned. Stir in the flour, then gradually add the wine, stirring until flour and liquid are smoothly blended.

Pour in the stock, add salt and pepper and heat to simmering point, then pour over the meat in the casserole. Add the thyme, then arrange the potato slices on top in an overlapping pattern. Season the potatoes with salt and pepper and dot the surface with another third of the butter. Cover with a lid or a double layer of foil and place in the oven. Cook for 2 hours.

After about 1½ hours, remove the lid or the foil and brush the potatoes with the remaining butter. Turn the temperature up to 200°C (400°F), Gas 6 and place the hotpot back in the oven, uncovered, for the last 30 minutes of cooking. Alternatively, heat the grill to high and place under the grill to crisp up. Remove from the oven or grill and serve.

Sliced duck breast with winter stir-fry

Serves 4

3 tbsp runny honey
2 large or 4 small duck breasts
Salt and black pepper

For the stir-fry
2 tbsp olive oil
150g (5oz) pancetta, diced
4 long shallots, peeled, halved lengthways (root left intact)
50–75g (2–3oz) butter
300g (11oz) Brussels sprouts, outer leaves removed and thinly sliced
8 brown cap mushrooms, sliced
300ml (11fl oz) beef or Chicken Stock (see page 216)
110g (4oz) pre-cooked chestnuts (see page 116), chopped
2 tbsp chopped flat-leaf parsley

This dish is full of strong, wintry flavours. For the best result, buy Brussels sprouts still on the stalk and crisp up the duck before baking to enhance the taste and texture.

Preheat the oven to 180°C (350°F), Gas 4. On the hob, heat a frying pan large enough to fry the duck breasts side by side, add the honey and allow to bubble gently. Season both sides of each duck breast with salt and pepper, place into the frying pan, skin side down, and cook gently over a medium heat until the duck is crisp and the honey has turned brown.

Transfer the duck breasts into a baking dish, skin side up. Bake in the oven for 8–10 minutes (longer for well done), then remove from the oven and set aside to rest for a few minutes before slicing.

Meanwhile, add half the olive oil to a non-stick frying pan set over a high heat and fry the pancetta until golden brown. Remove from the pan, dry on kitchen paper and set aside.

Drain off the fat from the pan, then set the pan back over the heat, add the rest of the oil and add the shallots to brown them. After they have been cooking for 2–3 minutes, melt half the butter in the pan and tip in the Brussels sprouts and mushrooms. Sauté for 4–5 minutes to brown a little, adding more butter if necessary, then add the cooked pancetta.

Pour in the stock and simmer to reduce for 2 minutes, then stir in the chestnuts and the rest of the butter. Add the parsley and season with salt and pepper. Place on plates and arrange the sliced duck on top.

Honey-glazed quail with beetroot, apple and hazelnut salad

Serves 4

175g (6oz) fresh beetroot
4 whole boneless quails
2 tbsp runny honey
4 sprigs of rosemary
1 bunch of thyme
2 tbsp olive oil
2 dessert apples
150g (5oz) mixed salad leaves
Salt and black pepper

For the dressing
2 tsp wholegrain mustard
25ml (1fl oz) white wine vinegar
50g (2oz) shelled hazelnuts, skinned (see page 30) and chopped
50ml (2fl oz) extra-virgin olive oil
25ml (1fl oz) hazelnut oil

Now that quails are commercially reared, they are becoming more and more popular in cooking. There are many ways of preparing them – in India I even had quail curry! Get your butcher to de-bone them for you, as they can be a bit fiddly.

To cook the beetroot for the salad, place in a large saucepan of cold water, add a good pinch of salt, bring to the boil and cook for 30–40 minutes. Allow to cool, then peel and set aside.

Preheat the oven to 180°C (350°F), Gas 4. Season each quail with salt and pepper and brush with the honey. Scatter the herbs in a large roasting tin and drizzle with the olive oil, then place the quails on top and bake in the oven for about 15 minutes, occasionally spooning over any juices that appear. When cooked, the quails should be golden brown but, when pricked with a fork, the juices should run a little red.

To make the dressing, place the mustard, vinegar and hazelnuts in a bowl. Mix together and then slowly add the olive oil and hazelnut oil, continuing to mix until combined. Season with salt and pepper, to taste, and pour into a sauce boat or jug.

Peel, core and chop the apples into cubes, chop the beetroot and mix both together with the salad leaves in a serving bowl.

Remove the quails from the oven, allow to rest for 5 minutes, then transfer to a serving plate. Drain the juices from the tin and pour them over the quails. Serve with the bowl of salad and jug of dressing.

Breaded pork chops with celeriac purée and herb spätzle

Serves 4

2 eggs
4 trimmed pork chops,
bone on, fat removed
150g (5oz) breadcrumbs
mixed with chopped
herbs (parsley, chives,
rosemary and thyme)
3–4 tbsp olive oil
25g (1oz) butter
2 sprigs of thyme, leaves
only, chopped
Salt and black pepper

For the celeriac purée
1 head of celeriac,
peeled and cut into
cubes
2 medium potatoes,
peeled
25g (1oz) butter

For the herb spätzle
500g (1lb 2oz) plain flour
4 eggs, beaten
2 tbsp double cream
1 tbsp chopped chives
1 tbsp chopped flat-leaf
parsley
1 tbsp chopped chervil
Pinch of salt

Spätzle are a German version of gnocchi or noodles. They are very easy to make and go excellently with most types of meat.

Beat the eggs gently in a bowl. Season the pork chops with salt and pepper and dip in the egg, then in the breadcrumb mixture, coating well. Put the chops on a plate in the fridge until needed.

Place the celeriac and potatoes in a large saucepan of salted water, bring to the boil and cook for 10–12 minutes. Drain, transfer to a blender, and mix to a purée, adding butter as the mixture begins to soften. Add a little salt, and set aside.

Bring a clean saucepan of salted water to the boil and prepare a separate bowl of iced water. Blend together all the ingredients for the spätzle in a bowl. With a spatula, spread a layer of the mixture on a chopping board. Cut into strips about 1cm (½in) wide and drop into the boiling water. Allow to cook for 2 minutes, then remove and plunge into the iced water.

Preheat the oven to 180°C (350°F), Gas 4. Set a non-stick ovenproof pan over a medium heat, with 1 tablespoon of olive oil. Drizzle more oil over the pork chops, place in the pan and fry on both sides until golden brown. Transfer the pan to the oven for 4–5 minutes. Keep basting the chops whilst on the hob and in the oven to ensure they stay moist. Meanwhile, set a non-stick frying pan over a medium heat and add the remaining oil, along with the butter and thyme. Remove the spätzle from the iced water and fry briefly. Drain and season with salt and pepper.

Remove the pork from the oven, season with salt and pepper and allow to rest for 2–3 minutes. Place the pork and spätzle on plates and serve with a dollop of celeriac purée.

Pork loin with sherry-roasted parsnips and chestnuts

Serves 4–6

2 kg (4lb 4oz) loin of pork
50g (2oz) butter
Salt and black pepper
½ bunch of watercress, to serve

For the parsnips and chestnuts
800g (1¾lb) parsnips, peeled and cut into 7.5cm (3in) batons
250ml (9fl oz) dry sherry, such as fino or manzanilla
75g (3oz) soft light brown sugar
110g (4oz) butter, cut into pieces
10 roasted chestnuts (see page 116), peeled and roughly chopped
1 bunch of flat-leaf parsley, chopped

It's important that there's plenty of fat when you're cooking this joint, so look for good-quality, free-range pork that has a decent coating of it. It will keep the meat moist while cooking and will also produce really good crackling.

Preheat the oven to 200°C (400°F), Gas 6.

Score the fat on the pork with a sharp knife and place in a roasting tin, season with salt and pepper and smother the fat with the butter. Bake in the oven for 1¼ hours, basting every 15 minutes to get the fat nice and crisp. Remove from the oven and allow to rest for 5 minutes before serving.

Meanwhile, place the parsnips in an ovenproof pan or roasting tin, add the sherry, sugar and butter and mix together to combine. Place in the oven for 15–20 minutes, or until golden and tender.

Remove the parsnips from the dish, then set the pan or tin over a high heat and reduce the liquid so that it evaporates, forming a glaze in the bottom of the pan. Place the parsnips back in the pan along with the chestnuts and parsley. Remove from the heat, season with salt and pepper and stir all the ingredients together.

To serve, remove the crackling from the pork and cut into pieces, then slice the meat. Place the parsnips and chestnuts on the centre of each serving plate, top with sliced pork, crackling and a handful of watercress.

Mango, coriander and apple chutney

Makes 1 litre (1¾ pints)
Vegetarian

1 large cooking apple
3 mangoes
225g (8oz) caster sugar
1 tsp mixed spice
½ tsp turmeric
1 tsp black mustard
seeds
½ green chilli
2 cloves of garlic, peeled
and finely chopped
1 onion, peeled and
finely chopped
1 tbsp finely chopped
root ginger
350ml (12fl oz) malt
vinegar
10g (½oz) coriander
leaves

This classic chutney from Goa is great served with curry.

Peel and core the apple, then peel the mangoes and cut the fruit on either side of the stone, removing the rest of the flesh around the stone with a small knife. Chop the mangoes and the apple into 1cm (½in) cubes and place into a bowl with the sugar and spices.

Add the mustard seeds, chilli, garlic, onion and ginger to the fruit mix, stir well together, cover the bowl and place in the fridge to infuse for 1 hour.

Remove from the fridge and tip into a large saucepan set over a medium heat, then pour in the vinegar. Bring to a simmer and cook for about 1 hour to thicken, add the coriander leaves and place in sterilised jars (see page 166). Properly sealed and stored in a cool, dark place, the chutney keeps for up to 6 months; once opened, store in the fridge for up to 1 week.

Spiced apple chutney

Makes 1 litre (1¾ pints)
Vegetarian

800g (1¾lb) cooking apples
50ml (2fl oz) extra-virgin olive oil
6 black peppercorns
300g (11oz) sultanas
110g (4oz) demerara sugar
400ml (14fl oz) cider vinegar
3½ tbsp chopped root ginger
1 tbsp sea salt
1 cinnamon stick, broken into large pieces
2 star anise
1 tsp freshly grated nutmeg
2 tbsp allspice

This is one of the chutneys I make at home every year, using apples from my garden. It's quick to make and any type of apple will do for it – whatever you have to hand. Serve it with white meat dishes or to accompany simple cheese on toast for breakfast.

Peel and core the apples and cut into 1cm (½in) cubes. Set a large saucepan over a medium heat and add the oil, along with the apples, peppercorns, sultanas and sugar, and fry until the fruit begins to caramelise.

Pour in the cider vinegar, raise the heat to high and boil for 1 minute. Then add the rest of the ingredients, bring back up to the boil, then reduce to a simmer and cook for 30 minutes until most of the liquid has evaporated. The chutney has a tendency to stick to the bottom of the pan so keep your eye on it while it's cooking.

Spoon it into sterilised jars (see page 166), filling them as full as you can, and seal while hot. Properly sealed and stored in a cool, dark place, the chutney keeps for up to 6 months; once opened, store in the fridge for up to 1 week.

Caramelised pear and almond strudel

Serves 6

**200g (7oz) granulated
sugar**

**1 vanilla pod, seeds
only**

**3–4 pears, peeled and
cut into 0.5cm (¼in)
slices**

**110g (4oz) flaked
almonds**

40g (1½oz) currants

40g (1½oz) sultanas

1 tsp ground cinnamon

**½ tsp freshly grated
nutmeg**

**4 sheets ready-made
filo pastry**

Flour, for dusting

**125g (4½oz) butter,
melted, plus extra for
greasing**

5 tbsp caster sugar

**75g (3oz) crème
fraîche, to serve**

*A strudel is traditionally shaped like a horseshoe, but you can
make it in whatever shape you like. Cherries, apples or peaches
also make great fillings. Just choose the fruit by the season.*

Preheat the oven to 180°C (350°F), Gas 4. Grease and line
a baking sheet with parchment paper.

Place the sugar and vanilla seeds in a heavy-based frying
pan, add 4 tablespoons of water and set over a low–medium
heat. Cook for 5–8 minutes, or until golden brown and
caramelised. Add the pears and almonds, along with the dried
fruit and spices, and cook for 10 minutes, or until the pear
slices are tender. Remove the pear mixture from the pan with
a slotted spoon and allow to cool to room temperature.

To prepare the strudel, place a sheet of filo pastry on a lightly
floured work surface, brush lightly with the melted butter
and sprinkle with 1 tablespoon of sugar, then add another
layer of pastry and repeat the process. Cover with two more
layers of pastry, then brush lightly with more of the butter.

Lay the pear mixture on one half of the pastry, leaving about
2cm (¾in) between the mixture and the nearest edge. Gently
fold the other half of the pastry over the top and tuck the long
edge under to create a log shape, brushing the edges with a
little butter and pressing together to seal. Brush the top of the
strudel with butter and sprinkle with the remaining sugar. Cut
the log in half and place on the baking sheet. Bake for 25–30
minutes, or until the pastry is golden brown and crispy.

Remove from the oven, allow to cool slightly and cut each
strudel into slices. Serve with dollops of crème fraîche.

Caramelised quince and Cox apple tart

Serves 4

2 quinces
75g (3oz) butter, melted
1 cinnamon stick
25–50g (1–2oz) caster sugar
450g (1lb) ready-made puff pastry
Flour, for dusting
6 Cox's Orange Pippin apples
3 tbsp icing sugar, for dusting
2 tbsp runny honey
Vanilla ice cream, to serve

The taste and texture of a quince is somewhere between an apple and a pear. In Middle Eastern cuisine, quinces are mostly used for savoury dishes – stews and stuffings. Here in Britain, quince sauce was the traditional accompaniment to roast partridge. I like this fruit best when used in desserts, such as in this delicious tart.

Peel and core the quinces and cut into 1 cm (½in) cubes, then place in a heavy-based saucepan with a lid along with a third of the butter and the cinnamon stick. Set over a low–medium heat and cook for 15–20 minutes, or until soft. Add sugar to taste, but leaving the quinces a little sharp.

Grease 1–2 large non-stick baking sheets. Roll out the puff pastry thinly on a lightly floured work surface and prick all over with a fork. Cut out 4 x 15–18cm (6–7in) diameter discs. (To do so, place a round cake tin or plate on the pastry and cut round it four times, re-rolling the pastry and cutting out again, as needed.) Carefully transfer to the baking sheets and place in the fridge for 30 minutes to rest.

Preheat the oven to 180°C (350°F), Gas 4. Peel and core the apples, cut in half, then cut into thin slices with a sharp knife. Remove the tart bases from the fridge. Heavily dust the edges of the pastry with icing sugar and spread the quince purée on the middle of each disc. Arrange the apple slices so that they fan out in a circle on top, drizzle with another third of the butter and with the honey and 25g (1oz) sugar and bake in the oven for 5–6 minutes, or until golden brown.

Remove from the oven, brush with the remaining butter and serve with a scoop of vanilla ice cream.

Christmas pudding ice cream with satsumas and caramel sauce

Serves 4
(Makes 500ml ice cream)

1 x 500ml tub vanilla ice cream
200g (7oz) Christmas pudding
2 tbsp brandy
200g (7oz) caster sugar, plus extra for sprinkling
1 vanilla pod, split
4 satsumas, peeled and cut in half widthways

To be honest, I'm not a big fan of Christmas pudding so I think this is a much better way to eat it. In any case, it's an ideal method for using up the leftovers. If you've bought a pudding especially for this recipe, first cook according to the instructions on the packet. Instead of the brandy, try Japanese yuzu juice (one capful would be enough), which is like essence of satsuma and mandarin – it really enhances the flavour!

Remove the ice cream from the freezer and allow to soften slightly for 5–10 minutes. Meanwhile, crumble the Christmas pudding into a mixing bowl and pour over the brandy. Allow to marinate for 10 minutes.

Take the ice cream and mix in the crumbled Christmas pudding, then place back in the freezer until required, removing 5–10 minutes before serving.

Preheat the oven to 180°C (350°F), Gas 4.

Pour the sugar into a non-stick saucepan and set on the hob over a medium heat. Allow to caramelise, then remove from the heat. Add the split vanilla pod and scraped-out seeds, then gradually add 50ml (2fl oz) water, stirring it in, and set aside.

Place the satsumas on a baking sheet, sprinkle with a little sugar and roast for 5–6 minutes. Remove from the oven and place in a serving dish. Pour over the caramel sauce and serve each with a scoop of the Christmas pudding ice cream.

Four-minute figgy pudding with custard

Serves 4

**110g (4oz) self-raising
  flour, sifted, plus
  extra for dusting**
110g (4oz) caster sugar
**110g (4oz) butter,
  softened, plus extra
  for greasing**
2 eggs
25ml (1fl oz) milk
**4 fresh figs or 110g
  (4oz) dried figs, finely
  chopped**
4 tbsp runny honey

For the custard
5 egg yolks
50g (2oz) caster sugar
150ml (5fl oz) milk
**250ml (9fl oz) double
  cream**
**1 vanilla pod, seeds
  only**

This popular winter pudding has been around since the sixteenth century, although, like Christmas, it was once banned by the Puritans. But it survived and can be cooked in loads of different ways – steamed, baked or even fried.

To make the sponge pudding, grease and lightly flour an ovenproof glass bowl – a 1.75 litre (3 pint) basin should do. Place the flour, sugar, butter, eggs and milk in a food processor, along with a quarter of the chopped figs, and mix to a smooth batter. Alternatively, add all the ingredients to a large bowl and mix using an electric beater.

Place the remaining figs in a bowl and mix in the honey. Spoon into the basin and pour the sponge mixture on top.

Wrap the top of the pudding basin with foil or greaseproof paper and tie with string. Place in a steamer or large saucepan half filled with water and steam over a low–medium heat for 1 hour. Alternatively, place some cling film over the top of the bowl, not touching the sponge mixture, and place in the microwave on a high setting for 4 minutes. When cooked, the pudding should be risen and just firm to the touch.

To make the custard, place the egg yolks and sugar in a bowl and whisk until blended. Place the milk, cream and vanilla seeds in a medium-sized saucepan and bring to the boil.

Once boiling, pour the hot milk over the eggs and whisk well, then return to the pan and cook slowly over a low heat to thicken, but don't boil it. Once thickened, pass through a sieve and pour into a serving jug, then carefully tip the sponge on to a serving plate.

Hot spiced cranberry punch

Makes 2 litres (3½ pints)

2 oranges
1 lemon
1 vanilla pod
1.5 litres (2½ pints)
  sweetened cranberry
  juice
500ml (18fl oz) red
  wine
8 whole cloves
175g (6oz) cranberries
250g (9oz) runny
  honey
2 cinnamon sticks,
  crushed
6 juniper berries

A wonderfully warming drink, this is a tangier alternative to traditional mulled wine.

Peel the oranges and lemon with a potato peeler (to retain as much of the pith and flavour as possible), then slice the fruit. Split the vanilla pod in half and scrape out the seeds, then place the pod and seeds and the orange and lemon slices in a large, heavy-based saucepan. Add the remaining ingredients, set the pan over a medium heat and gently warm for about 20 minutes. This will allow everything to infuse and the cranberries to cook. Serve warm.

Stocks, sauces and dressings

French dressing

Makes 450ml (16fl oz)
Vegetarian

250ml (9fl oz) rapeseed or
  extra-virgin olive oil
110ml (4fl oz) white wine
  vinegar

Juice of 1 lemon
Pinch of sugar
Salt and black pepper

Whisk all the ingredients (except salt and pepper) in a bowl.
Season with salt and pepper and store in a clean jar with a lid.
Keep for up to 1 week and shake vigorously before use.

Vinaigrette

Makes 450ml (16fl oz)
Vegetarian

300ml (11fl oz) extra-virgin
  olive oil
3 tbsp white or red wine
  vinegar
1 tbsp Dijon mustard

2 small shallots, peeled and
  finely chopped
25g (1oz) flat-leaf parsley,
  finely chopped
Salt and black pepper

Whisk all the ingredients (except the salt and pepper) together
in a bowl. Season with salt and pepper and store in a clean
jar with a lid. Store in the fridge for up to 1 week and shake
vigorously before use.

Mint sauce

A classic accompaniment for lamb.

Makes 400ml (14fl oz), Vegetarian

50g (2oz) mint leaves,
  chopped
25g (1oz) caster sugar

150ml (5fl oz) malt vinegar
Salt and black pepper

Place the mint leaves and sugar in a bowl, pour over
4 tablespoons of hot water and leave for 3 minutes. Add
the vinegar, season with salt and pepper and mix together
well. Store in the fridge for up to 1 week

Creamed horseradish

Delicious served alongside beef or mackerel.

Makes 400ml (14fl oz), Vegetarian

300ml (11fl oz) double
  cream
110g (4oz) finely grated
  fresh horseradish

Juice of 1 lemon
Salt and black pepper

Pour the cream into a bowl and whisk until soft peaks are
formed. Stir in the grated horseradish, followed by the lemon
juice, a little at a time, and season with salt and pepper.
Store in the fridge for up to 4–5 days.

Mayonnaise

The best mayo is a homemade version, served when fresh.

Makes 1 litre (1¾ pints), Vegetarian

6 egg yolks
¼ tsp salt
1½ tbsp white wine vinegar
½ tbsp English mustard

1 litre (1¾ pints) rapeseed
** or vegetable oil**
Salt and black pepper

Whisk the egg yolks, salt, vinegar and mustard together in a clean bowl, then very slowly add the oil until it has all been incorporated. If the mayonnaise is too thick, add 1–2 tablespoons of warm water. Season with salt and pepper and store in the fridge for 3–4 days.

Quick Hollandaise sauce

A great sauce to put with egg dishes or tender asparagus stalks.

Makes 250ml (9fl oz), Vegetarian

2 egg yolks
Juice of ½ lemon
225g (8oz) butter, melted

Good pinch of cayenne
** pepper**
¾ tsp salt

Mix the egg yolks, lemon juice and 2 tablespoons of water in a blender, or place in a bowl and mix the ingredients using an electric beater. Slowly incorporate the butter into the mixture, pouring only the clear melted butter into the mixture and leaving any milk solids in the pan, then season with cayenne pepper and salt. Serve freshly made.

Tartar sauce

The traditional sauce to accompany all types of fish.

Makes 500ml (18fl oz), Vegetarian

3 egg yolks
2 tbsp cider vinegar
300ml (11fl oz) vegetable oil
110g (4oz) capers
150g (5oz) gherkins,
  chopped

½ shallot, peeled and finely
  chopped
½ bunch of dill, chopped
2 tbsp chopped flat-leaf
  parsley
Juice of ½ lemon
Salt and black pepper

To make the tartar sauce, whisk together the egg yolks and vinegar in a bowl. Still whisking, start adding the vegetable oil very slowly to make a mayonnaise. The mixture should be thick and light once the oil is incorporated.

Stir in the capers, gherkins, shallot and herbs. Season with salt and pepper and add the lemon juice, then set aside. Store for up to 3 days in the fridge.

Chicken stock

Makes about 1.5 litres
(2½ pints)

1 tbsp olive oil
1kg (2lb 2oz) chicken
   bones, chopped up
   and with all skin
   removed
2 small onions, peeled
   and chopped
110g (4oz) carrots,
   peeled and chopped
½ head of garlic (garlic
   head chopped in half
   widthways and skin
   left on)
1 leek, chopped
2 sticks of celery,
   chopped
1 tsp black peppercorns
1 bay leaf
3 sprigs of thyme

Chicken stock is a staple – it's used in so many recipes to add flavour. I haven't included a recipe for beef stock in this book – I tend not to make it from scratch as it takes too long, so use a good-quality, fresh, store-bought version, or replace with chicken stock as an excellent alternative.

Pour the olive oil into a large, heavy-based saucepan set over a medium heat, add the chicken bones and allow to brown, scraping the bottom of the pan with a wooden spoon from time to time to dislodge any pieces that get stuck.

Add the remaining ingredients and allow to cook for 2–3 minutes, then pour in 2 litres (3½ pints) water. Bring to the boil, skimming off any scum that floats to the surface, then reduce the heat and simmer gently for 1½ hours.

Remove from the heat and allow to cool slightly, then pass through a sieve, discarding the bones and reserving the liquid. If you prefer a stronger-tasting stock, pour the liquid back into the pan and simmer to reduce by half. Store the stock in the fridge in an airtight container for 3–4 days or place in the freezer.

Fish stock

*Makes about 1.2 litres
(2 pints)*

*Another essential stock recipe – particularly useful for fish-based
stews and risottos.*

2 tbsp olive oil
**110g (4oz) onions,
  peeled and chopped**
1 small leek, chopped
**1 clove of garlic, peeled
  and crushed**
**1 stick of celery,
  chopped**
**500g (1lb 2oz)
  chopped fish bones
  (such as sole, whiting,
  halibut, brill)**
2 sprigs of thyme
**½ bunch of flat-leaf
  parsley**
**1 tsp black
  peppercorns**
1 bay leaf

Add the oil to a large, heavy-based saucepan set over a
medium heat, then tip in the vegetables and cook for 2–3
minutes. Add the fish bones and herbs and cook for a further
2–3 minutes.

Pour in 1.5 litres (2½ pints) water and bring to the boil,
skimming off any scum that floats to the surface. Add the
peppercorns and bay leaf, reduce the heat and simmer for
20 minutes.

Remove from the heat and allow to cool slightly, then pass
through a fine sieve, discarding the bones and reserving the
liquid. Store the stock in the fridge in an airtight container
for 3–4 days or place in the freezer.

Vegetable stock

Makes about 1.2 litres
(2 pints)
Vegetarian

1 tbsp olive oil
2 cloves of garlic,
  peeled and crushed
2 onions, peeled and
  chopped
3 carrots, peeled and
  chopped
1 leek, chopped
3 sticks of celery,
  chopped
½ head of fennel,
  chopped
3 sprigs of fresh thyme
1 sprig of fresh
  rosemary
2 bay leaves
1 tsp white
  peppercorns
1 glass of white wine
1 lemon, sliced

A great way to use up all your leftover vegetables and add flavour to vegetarian dishes.

Add the olive oil to a large, heavy-based saucepan set over a medium heat, then tip in the vegetables and cook for 2–3 minutes.

Add the herbs and peppercorns and cook for a further 2–3 minutes, then add the wine and continue to cook for 3 minutes. Pour in 1.5 litres (2½ pints) water, bring to the boil, reduce the heat and simmer for 15 minutes.

Remove the pan from the heat, add the sliced lemon and allow to cool completely. Strain through a fine sieve, discarding the vegetables and reserving the liquid. Store the stock in the fridge in an airtight container for 2–3 days or place in the freezer.

Supplier list

Fish

Island Seafare Ltd
Tim and Paddy Croft produce brilliant fresh and smoked seafood. Their produce is available online.

The Quay, Port Saint Mary, Isle of Man, IM9 5EA
+44(0)1624 834494
www.islandseafare.co.uk

R.J & E.G Noble
Based near Whitby and established over 100 years ago, these guys stock excellent crab and shellfish.

Unit 2C, Fairfield Way, Whitby, North Yorkshire, YO22 4PU
+44(0)1947 820413
www.starcrosswhitby.com/nobles_website/

Fortunes Smokehouse and Kipper shop
In my opinion, the best kippers you can buy. Full stop.

Henrietta Street, Whitby, North Yorkshire, YO22 4DW
+44(0)1947 601659

Iain R. Spink
Iain produces original Arbroath Smokies – haddock which has been salted and smoked to a delicious golden-brown finish.

+44(0)1241 860303
www.arbroathsmokies.net

St Mawes fish shop
A fantastic fish shop right on the quay in the village of St Mawes, Cornwall. The fish is caught by local fisherman Pete Green. Opening times vary depending on the season, so look online for details.

+44(0)7792 220821
www.stmawesseafood.co.uk

The Whitstable Fish Market
South Quay, The Harbour, Whitstable, Kent, CT5 1AB
+44(0)1227 771245
www.seewhitstable.com/Whitstable-Fish-Market.html

Latimers Shellfish Deli
Visit the shop or look online for delicious, fresh shellfish and other types of fish.

Shell Hill, Bents Road, Whitburn, Tyne & Wear, SR6 7NT
+44(0)191 5292200
www.latimers.com

Meat

Colin M. Robinson
Colin is my favourite butcher. He runs two stores, which sell brilliant lamb and quality meat. You can also purchase online.

41, Main Street, Grassington, Skipton, North Yorkshire, BD23 5AA
+44(0)1756 752476
www.britnett-carver.co.uk/robinsonsbutchers/

Greenfield Pork Products
Supplier Martin Martindale offers superb free-range pork, bacon and sausages from his family-run Hampshire business, with its herd of specialist pigs.

Sunnycliff, Highbury Road, Anna Valley, Andover, Hampshire, SP11 7LU
+44(0)1264 359422
www.greenfield-pork.co.uk

Laverstoke Park Farm
An amazing, one-of-a-kind farm, offering everything from meat to vegetables, milk and cheese (the mozzarella comes highly recommended). Order online or visit the farm shop.

Overton, Hampshire, RG25 3DR
+44(0)1256 772813
www.laverstokepark.co.uk

Donald Russell
An excellent Scottish butcher and meat supplier, which also sells great salmon. Purchases can be made from the website.

Harlaw Road, Inverurie, Aberdeenshire, AB51 4FR
+44(0)1467 629666
www.donaldrussell.com

Piper Farm
A family-run Devonshire farm, winner of a BBC Best Food Producer award. They rear all their own produce, which can be bought from their Exeter shop or from their website.

Cullompton, Devon, EX15 1SD
+44(0)1392 881380
www.pipersfarm.com

Broad Stripe Butchers
An online gourmet butcher with an excellent range of meat.

Fairfax Meadow, 6 Newmarket Drive, Osmaston Park Estate, Derby, DE24 8SW
+44(0)800 0911518
www.broadstripebutchers.co.uk

Vicars Game
A Berkshire-based butchers and game dealers specialising in quality English meat and game.

Casey Fields Farm, Dog Lane, Ashampstead, Reading, Berkshire, RG8 8SJ
+44(0)1635 579662
www.vicarsgame.co.uk

M. Moen & Sons
A top-quality London butcher.

24, The Pavement, Clapham Common, London, SW4 0JA
+44(0)20 76221624
www.moen.co.uk

Vegetables

Conrad Davies' Spar
A local food hero, joint winner of the BBC Best Local Food Retailer award in 2008.

Y Maes, Pwllheli, Gwynedd, Wales, LL53 5HA
+44(0)1758 612993

Bury Market
This is one of my favourite UK markets; for food lovers it is definitely worth a visit. It's closed on Sundays.

Bury town centre
+44(0)161 2536520
www.burymarket.com

Calon Wen Organic Foods
This farmers' co-operative supplies great organic fruit and veg.

Unit 4, Whitland Industrial Estate, Whitland, Camarthenshire, SA34 0HR
+44(0)1994 241368
www.calonwen.co.uk

Whole Foods Market
A huge multi-storey food hall in West London. A good place to find premium and unusual produce.

The Barkers Building, 63–97, Kensington High Street, London, W8 5SE
+44(0)20 73684500
www.wholefoodsmarket.com

Fenwick
Newcastle's department store has a highly-respected food hall which promotes its local suppliers.

Northumberland Street, Newcastle upon Tyne, NE99 1AR
+44(0)191 2325100
www.fenwick.co.uk

Hampshire Farmers' Markets
With locations all over the county, these are my local markets – I highly recommend them. Check online for dates and locations.

+44(0)1420 588671
www.hampshirefarmersmarkets.co.uk

The Garlic Farm
The UK's premier grower of garlic and a source of all things garlic-related, based on the Isle of Wight. Buy online from their website.

Mersley Lane, Newchurch, Isle of Wight, PO36 0NR
+44(0)1983 865378
www.thegarlicfarm.co.uk

Continued overleaf…

Deli, Bakery & Dairy

Valvona & Crolla
A great deli in the heart of Edinburgh. Visit the shop, café or website.

19, Elm Row, Edinburgh, EH7 4AA
+44 (0)131 5566066
www.valvonacrolla.co.uk

London Fine Foods
A great online store that supplies top restaurants and the public with luxury food via the web.

Unit D175, New Covent Garden Market, London, SW8 5LL
+44 (0)845 6439121
www.efoodies.co.uk

Neal's Yard Dairy
The highly-respected London dairy. Either shop online or visit their shops in Borough Market and Covent Garden.

108, Druid Street, London, SE1 2HH
+44 (0)20 75007520
www.nealsyarddairy.co.uk

Tom's Deli
226 Westbourne Grove, Notting Hill, London
+44 (0)20 72218818
www.tomsdelilondon.co.uk

Cadogan and James Deli
The Square, Winchester, Hampshire, SO23 9EX
+44 (0)1962 840805

Paul Hollywood Bread
Paul is one of the best-known UK bakers – his artisan breads are among the best.

Unit 19, Miners Way Business Park, Ackholt Road, Aylesham, Kent, CT3 3AJ
+44 (0)1304 841115
www.paulhollywood.com

Jeroboams
London's largest independent wine merchant – also a great place to buy artisan cheese.

7–9, Elliott's Place, London, N1 8HX
+44 (0)20 7288 8850
www.jeroboams.co.uk

Mey Selections
Suppliers of high-quality farm and food products sourced from the North Scottish Highlands.

North Highland Products Ltd., 34a High Street, Wick, Caithness, KW1 4BS
+44 (0)845 8380488
www.mey-selections.com

Fresh Basil
A great deli in the heart of Derbyshire.

23 Strutt Street, Belper, Derbyshire, DE56 1UN
+44 (0)1773 828882

Uncle Henry's
This farm shop is a great place to browse for meats, cheeses and veg.

Grayingham Grange Farm, Grayingham, Gainsborough, Lincolnshire, DN21 4JD
+44 (0)1652 640308
www.unclehenrys.co.uk

Betty's Tea Rooms
With several locations in and around Yorkshire, you can pop in to a Betty's or shop online for delicious products.

+44 (0)1423 814000
www.bettys.co.uk

Acknowledgements

First, I'd like to thank my mother, sister and Peter for being there through the good times and the bad – I love you so much. To my agents, Fiona, Alison and Mary, for the never-ending work you guys seem to do. To all the girls at HarperCollins – Jenny, Ione and all the crew – thank you so much for the best book yet. I feel at home with you guys, you're all brilliant. Pippa, cheers for your diary-filling, and Chris, you're on the turn mate – another one of these and I'll be calling you a home economist! And, finally, my mate Fudge the dog – he won't read this, so I'm off now to give him a bone.

Index

First published in 2009 by Collins
HarperCollins Publishers Ltd.
77–85 Fulham Palace Road
London W6 8JB
www.harpercollins.co.uk

Text © James Martin, 2009
Photographs © Jonathan Gregson, 2009

13 12 11 10 09
10 9 8 7 6 5 4 3 2 1

James Martin asserts his moral right to be identified as the author of this work.
All rights reserved. No parts of this publication may be reproduced, stored in a
retrieval system or transmitted, in any form or by any means, electronic, mechanical,
photocopying, recording or otherwise, without the prior permission of the publishers.
A catalogue record for this book is available from the British Library

ISBN   978 0 00 729470 1

Editorial Director: Jenny Heller
Project Editor: Ione Walder
Copy Editor: Kate Parker
Photography: Jonathan Gregson
Design Concept: Allies Design
Design Layout: Colin Hall

Colour reproduction by Butler Tanner and Dennis
Printed and bound in Great Britain by Butler Tanner and Dennis, Frome, Somerset